Dying to Be Free

How America's Ruling Class Is Killing and Bankrupting Americans, and What to Do About It

Leland Stillman, MD

May, 2022

Dedication:
To all those who would rather risk their lives than sacrifice their liberties, I salute you.

To all those who have stood watch so that I could have the freedom to become a doctor and to write this book, you have my deepest gratitude.

1. Dying to Be Free

How America's Public Health Policies Are Killing and Bankrupting Americans

"Give me liberty, or give me death!"

- Patrick Henry

Americans today are dying for want of freedom. Despite being told over and over again that they are free, the truth is that Americans have little freedom left. This is due to the rise of an oligarchy of technocrats who now rule our society in violation of the Constitution and the Bill of Rights. I call these people totalitarian technocrats, because they seek complete control over individuals and therefore society under the guise of "public health and safety." Every freedom we are now denied, is denied to us for the sake of protecting us from ourselves and from our fellow Americans. We have recently reached what I believe will be the high-watermark of this technocracy – forced vaccination. I believe that if anything threatens the health of the American people, it is the evil agenda of these technocrats, whether they are pushing mask-wearing, vaccination, water-fluoridation, or even things as innocuous as hand-washing. As much as it may surprise you to hear this from a doctor, my reasons for concern are based on an abundance of evidence and experience, and are shared by doctors and scientists all over the world.

I decided to write this book after watching the health of my country deteriorate over the course of my life. During that time, despite spending an ever increasing amount of money on health, the health of most Americans has deteriorated. Americans spent $1.4 trillion dollars or 13.3% of gross domestic product, on healthcare in 1996. They spent $3.1 trillion dollars or 17.9% of GDP, on healthcare in 2016.[1] What did they get for this vast sum of money? Their life expectancy has begun to decline over a similar period.[2] The budget

---

[1] Dieleman JL, Cao J, Chapin A, et al. US Health Care Spending by Payer and Health Condition, 1996-2016. JAMA. 2020;323(9):863–884.

[2] Venkataramani AS, O'Brien R, Tsai AC. Declining Life Expectancy in the United

for the National Institutes of Health is \$51.96 billion[3] the CDC \$15.4 billion[4] the FDA \$6.5 billion[5] Book after book has been written about corruption and incompetence at these agencies, and yet not a single agency or government employee guilty of malfeasance has been prosecuted, let alone sent to jail.[6,7,8,91011] No one has even been fired, or even politely let go, as a result of these allegations. The institutions of America's public health establishment are completely unaccountable, even as the facade of their competence crumbles into oblivion. Many people are quick to blame the ring-leaders, like Anthony Fauci, for this crisis, but the problem runs much, much deeper than that. The American public health establishment is rotten to its core. Their beliefs about public health are based on lies masquerading as science that have been foisted upon them and the world by the pharmaceutical industry.[12,13,14] As the health of the average American declines, these shameless bureaucrats continue to congratulate themselves despite their obvious failure. This fact leads us to the inescapable conclusion that the people in charge of American healthcare are some combination of incompetent, insane, and corrupt. The emperor has no clothes and I am not afraid to say it.

Despite the undeniable failure of our public health establishment to maintain the public health, we are told that the answer is to surrender more of our liberties and more of our wealth to exactly the experts who have failed to protect it. We are told that the answer to our public health woes is more government, more experts, more rules, more public health funding, and fewer rights, liberties, and freedoms.

States: The Need for Social Policy as Health Policy. JAMA. 2021;325(7):621–622.

3   https://officeofbudget.od.nih.gov

4   https://www.cdc.gov/media/releases/2021/s0528-fiscal-year-2022.html#:~:text=When%20accounting%20for%20all%20resources,of%20%2415.4%20billion%20for%20CDC.

5   https://www.fda.gov/news-events/congressional-testimony/presidents-fy2022-budget-request-fda-06102021#:~:text=Today%2C%20I%20am%20pleased%20to,the%20FY%202021%20Enacted%20level.

6   Holland, Mary, Kim Mack Rosenberg, and Eileen Iorio. *The HPV vaccine on trial: seeking justice for a generation betrayed.* Simon and Schuster, 2018.

7   Barry, Kevin. *Vaccine Whistleblower: exposing autism research fraud at the CDC.* Simon and Schuster, 2015.

8   Angell, M. (1997). *Science on trial: the clash of medical evidence and the law in the breast implant case.* WW Norton & Company.

9   Grundvig, James Ottar. *Master manipulator: The explosive true story of fraud, embezzlement, and government betrayal at the CDC.* Skyhorse, 2016.

10   Kennedy Jr., Robert F. *The Real Anthony Fauci.* Simon and Schuster, 2021.

11   Mikovits, J., & Heckenlively, K. (2021). *Plague of Corruption: restoring faith in the promise of science.* Simon and Schuster.

12   Smith, Richard. "The trouble with medical journals." *Journal of the Royal Society of Medicine* 99, no. 3 (2006): 115-119.

13   Ioannidis, John PA. "Why most published research findings are false." *PLoS medicine* 2, no. 8 (2005): e124.

14   Angell, Marcia. *The truth about the drug companies: How they deceive us and what to do about it.* Random House Incorporated, 2005.

Anyone blessed with common sense can see that more of the same is only going to make America's health problems worse. The reason why is as simple as it is obvious. Americans are dying in record numbers because their government is restricting their rights. They are dying because the people who are really destroying the health of the American people - large corporations and government welfare programs - continue to grow more powerful, no matter who is elected to public office. Many poor and unhealthy Americans are foolishly voting for these policies, like addicts shoveling cocaine up their noses or mainlining heroin into their veins. Day by day, Americans find themselves stretched more thinly in the pursuit of happiness. They are less and less able to afford what they know makes them healthy. They are left with fewer and fewer healthy choices, until finally they resort to making unhealthy choices. There is a growing sense of fear and anxiety that the American dream – of hard work turning into fortune enough to afford a life of leisure and luxury – is turning into an American nightmare, in which we work as hard as we can to earn just enough to meet our most basic needs, but never enough to get ahead.

The Economic War on the American People

This is all by design. Over the past several decades, American corporations have steadily corrupted the democratic process to control more and more of American life. These corporations sell Americans products and services that are clearly unhealthy, and then do everything possible to silence anyone who will tell the truth about their products. They also do everything they can to transfer your tax dollars into their pockets through government subsidies, tax breaks, and other incentives. Politicians are only too happy to enrich themselves by acting as the intermediaries for these transactions.

Meanwhile, the small business owner and the family farmer – the bedrock of the American economy – have been economically decimated by these policies. This is but a part of the design to destroy the republic. By destroying the family farm and the small business, corporations have eliminated their competition. Farm debt in 2019 was $416 billion - an all-time high. More than half of all farmers have lost money every year since 2013.[15] The suicide rate for farmers is over double that of veterans.[16] Physicians and nurses are also at increased risk of suicide relative to the general public.[17] Male physicians have

---

15   https://time.com/5736789/small-american-farmers-debt-crisis-extinction/
16   www.theguardian.com/us-news/2017/dec/06/why-are-americas-farmers-killing-themselves-in-record-numbers
17   Davidson, J. E., Proudfoot, J., Lee, K., & Zisook, S. (2019). Nurse suicide in the United States: analysis of the Center for Disease Control 2014 national violent death reporting system dataset. Archives of psychiatric nursing, 33(5), 16-21.

a suicide rate 1.4 times the general public, and female physicians 2.27 times.[18]

What kind of country tolerates this level of suicide in its most essential workers and professionals? How can we possibly afford a catastrophically high physician suicide rate when we are in the middle of a historic healthcare-worker shortage?

The American government is waging full-out economic warfare upon the American people. It has become so grievous that now they are labeling everyday Americans as "extremists" for advocating for the preservation of their Constitutional rights. The true extremists are those who refuse to admit that their totalitarian and socialist policies are killing Americans left, right, and center. These extremists walk the halls of power in this nation with impunity, while their victims – hard-working, red-blooded Americans – struggle to afford the basic necessities of life.

The purpose of this book is to reveal just how depraved modern American healthcare policies have become, to explain how simple it is to ensure good health, and to prove why there is never any excuse to restrict people's liberties when it comes to their health decisions. This book will dismantle the mainstream healthcare narrative that is failing to protect and preserve the health, wealth, and liberty of modern Americans. The answer to the American healthcare crisis is not more government, more rules, more regulations, or more mandates, it is the return of our rights and liberties from the petty tyrants who have stolen them.

Freedom Is Vital to Good Health

The premise of this book is that freedom is the bedrock of the good health that Americans not long ago enjoyed. Why is freedom so essential to good health? Why are so-called health "experts" doomed to failure? Or perhaps doomed to corruption? How did we get here? How is it that we know more about health and the human body than ever before in history, and yet we have a healthcare crisis? This is a story that has repeated itself time and again throughout history. This is just the latest iteration.

What separates us from the rest of life on earth is our enormous brain and our opposable thumbs. These two things enable us to radically alter our world. We can turn deserts into lush forests, we can turn mountains into dust, we can dive to the depths of the oceans, and we can even soar into the sky.

18   Schernhammer, Eva S., and Graham A. Colditz. "Suicide rates among physicians: a quantitative and gender assessment (meta-analysis)." American Journal of Psychiatry 161, no. 12 (2004): 2295-2302.

We are obsessed with doing the impossible, with breaking records and defying nature to gain ever greater freedom of action. Freedom is our highest and most romanticized ideal. This begins with freedom from our basic wants and needs as living beings – our most basic want and need is to be free of disease.

We are obsessed with eliminating the discomforts and dangers that have, for most of our history, done us the most harm. These are basic threats to our survival, such as starvation, dehydration, hyper or hypothermia, blood loss, and overwhelming infections. We have done everything we can imagine to eliminate these threats to our well-being. We have created a world in which potable water comes out of every tap and a thermostat controls the temperature of our homes, offices, and cars. Emergency medical services are available sometimes in a matter of minutes to stop bleeding, rehydrate the dehydrated, warm the hypothermic, cool the hyperthermic, feed the starving, and annihilate infections with a formidable arsenal of anti-bacterials, anti-virals, anti-fungals, and anti-parasitics.

Within the borders of civilization, these threats have been minimized as far as humanly possible. And yet as we have conquered these ancient adversaries, we have seen the rise of diseases of civilization to replace them. Instead of hunger and starvation, we have epidemics of obesity and diabetes. The metabolically unfit (obese and/or diabetic) then become vulnerable to infections, even to the point of exhausting our extensive array of antibiotics due to antibiotic resistance. Instead of thirst and dehydration, people are frequently over-hydrated or are poisoning themselves with soft drinks, energy drinks, creamers, sweeteners, and so on. Instead of hypothermia and hyperthermia, people live in climate-controlled buildings and rarely have to break a sweat to cool off or shiver to keep warm. Yet sweating and shivering both have health benefits, and eliminating them from our lives has certainly led to increases in chronic diseases. Let me be very clear – stresses like fasting, sweating, shivering, exercise, breath-holding, and even the seemingly inconsequential act of chewing all have a positive impact on our health.[19] They are, in fact, indispensable to good health. Free people experience these stresses and, therefore, enjoy good health. Modern socialists are working hard to eliminate these stresses, and this is destroying the public's health. The modern public health establishment is composed almost exclusively of socialists – there is hardly a single friend of capitalism and freedom left within their ranks. Their approach is one of centralized authority (totalitarian technocracy) over individual autonomy. Their approach has obviously failed, as is clearly demonstrated by the failing health of the American people.

19   Watanabe, Y., Okada, K., Kondo, M., Matsushita, T., Nakazawa, S., & Yamazaki, Y. (2020). Oral health for achieving longevity. Geriatrics & gerontology international, 20(6), 526-538.

Freedom is the bedrock of strength and good health, but the enemies of freedom are quick to argue that, when left to their own devices, people often choose a slovenly, indulgent lifestyle. People do not want to do the hard work or exercise the self-control that is necessary to be healthy. They wrongly conclude that the solution, therefore, is to deprive people of their rights and force them to be healthy. They think that the answer to our ill health is another government program, another rule, another law, another mandate, or another regulation. Their justification for depriving people of their rights is that people do not truly want to be healthy, and, moreover, that they do not want to protect the health of others either.

This is a bold-faced lie. The fact is that Americans love to do what makes them healthy. They love to cook, hunt, fish, exercise, and garden. Every classic American past-time is a healthy pursuit. Why, then, are Americans unhealthy?

The vast majority of Americans today struggling with chronic illness are sick because their government has enabled and incentivized them, and corporations have influenced and seduced them into making unhealthy choices. Food subsidies are perhaps the most evil of these examples. This starts with adjusting the price of food. The government heavily subsidizes the most unhealthy foods that Americans eat. The number one and two purchases with food stamps are junk food and soda.[20] Meat, grain, and vegetable oils would all be far, far more expensive if the government did not heavily subsidize their production.[21] This is why a grass-fed steak bought at a farmer's market might cost you twice what a grain-fed steak might cost you at the grocery store. This system enriches corporations and their political pets (more often referred to as "elected officials"), while poisoning and impoverishing millions of Americans.

Once Americans fall ill, they are ushered into a healthcare system that does nothing to address their poor health choices. They are started on prescription medications that multiply as one after another is prescribed to control side effects of the previous prescriptions. No meaningful dietary or lifestyle changes are seriously pursued to prevent, mitigate, let alone reverse disease. Patients are referred to one sub-specialist after another, until they have more doctors, prescriptions, and medical appointments than they can keep track of. Shortly thereafter, they run out of money, leaving them destitute and reliant upon Medicare and Medicaid for their healthcare, Social Security for their spending money, and food stamps for their food.

---

20   https://www.nytimes.com/2017/01/13/well/eat/food-stamp-snap-soda.html
21   Mozaffarian, D., Rogoff, K. S., & Ludwig, D. S. (2014). The real cost of food: can taxes and subsidies improve public health?. JAMA, 312(9), 889–890.

Why Medical Doctors Are Paid to Fail

"Doctors are men who pour drugs of which they know little into patients of whom they know less to treat diseases of which they know nothing."

- Voltaire

In most cases, what is actually needed to restore the patient to good health is for the doctor to deliver the often unwelcome message of, "you need to eat healthier food than you have been eating," or, "you need to go to bed at a reasonable hour, get some exercise, get up off of the couch and go outside on a regular basis," and so on. The vast majority of patients rarely, if ever, get such vital messages from their doctors, because their doctors are not rewarded for delivering such messages. Doctors are paid the same regardless of how healthy their patients are. It is the only profession in the world where failure is rewarded for mediocrity, or even outright failure. The sad fact is that many doctors make more money as their patients become increasingly ill – they are paid to fail. Cardiologists and cardiothoracic surgeons get paid to treat heart attacks, not to prevent them. Gastroenterologists get paid to perform colonoscopies, not to prevent the need for colonoscopies. Nephrologists get paid to perform dialysis once a patient's kidneys have failed. Surgeons get paid to operate – not to prevent the need for operations. General practitioners, such as myself, are usually not paid by insurance companies based on how healthy we keep our patients. The sicker the patient, the more complex the case, and the more we "do," the more money we make. We do not make more money if we get our patients better. Or at least, insurance companies do not pay us more for better performance. They are, effectively, paying us to fail.

I, and all of the best doctors I know, refuse to settle for this level of mediocrity. Our patients pay us directly, for our time, just as they would pay any other highly qualified, trained, and valuable professional. I think that the best doctors work on retainer, but that is a discussion for later. At the end of the day, the vast majority of doctors in America are being paid to fail. The sicker the patients and the more care they need, the more money doctors, hospitals, and clinics make. Until doctors are incentivized to get patients better, patients should expect to only get worse. While there are certainly many corrupt and evil people to blame for this state of affairs, we must also acknowledge that it is the American people who ultimately decide what happens in their own country. They must come to grips with the fact that they are being ruthlessly exploited by the healthcare system that threatens to bankrupt them.

America's medical system is organized around failure, rather than success. No one should be surprised that in a system where failure is rewarded, failure is assured. We have trained entire generations of doctors who are paid to fail to get their patients better. The only exceptions to this are critical care and emergency surgery. No one gets paid if the patient dies, and it is when life and death are on the line that modern medicine and the American medical system actually excel. This has in turn driven doctors to specialize and practice only in the acute setting – the ICU, the hospital ward, the operating room – and has left America with a historic shortage of primary care doctors. Patients constantly complain that, "no one will listen to me," or, "my doctor doesn't take enough time with me," or "my doctor is always in such a rush." This is not how doctors wish to be – it is how the system has trained (paid) them to be.

The Failure of Public Health "Experts"

Public health "experts" and many doctors will quickly say that patients do not want to pay for preventative care, but this is nonsense. Doctors like me make even more money than our sub-specialist colleagues precisely because we are willing to take the time to prevent disease, long before it arises, and to correct it once it has. I and many other doctors in America are proof that freedom – not socialized medicine - is the answer to our healthcare woes, by keeping our patients happy and healthy, without billing their insurance companies or the government. If I were free to, I could insure every American for less than they currently insure their car. There is no reason for your monthly health insurance premium to be more than the cost of a single meal at a nice restaurant – it's just a matter of what you're buying. The insurance industry will never offer this kind of product, because they are making too much money rigging the game against you. That is why you have dozens of companies who will happily insure your car or house tomorrow, but only one or two options to insure your health, and you have to opt into the product at specific times of year. This is absurd. The government won't let anyone offer a superior health insurance product, because your elected officials are for sale and large insurance companies can easily buy them. We will discuss the problems of insurance companies and socialized medicine in greater detail later.

The people in charge of American healthcare have no incentive to fix the system. Just look at how wealthy it is making them. Modern healthcare is so profitable that the average pharmaceutical company listed on the S&P 500 is twice as profitable as its competitors in other industries. Twice as profitable? And people think that freedom is the problem? Freedom is not the problem.

Corporate greed and political corruption are the problem. In the past year, the response to COVID-19 has minted almost 500 new billionaires.[22] These people will shamelessly amass fortunes even as their countrymen and women struggle to make ends meet. These psychopaths are turning our republic into a dystopian disaster – it's time to stop complying with their agenda.

We have few freedoms left that are essential to our health and well-being. Americans are not free to buy and sell fresh, local foods like raw milk to one another. We are not free to buy and sell medical services - these all depend upon capricious standards of medical licensure. Your license can be taken without any due process by a state medical board, even if you have done nothing to endanger a patient. Americans are not free to buy and sell health insurance, which is why we have only one or two insurance companies for the entire nation. We are not free to choose what kind of food our tax dollars are spent to subsidize. We are not free to choose even what we see on our own media. It is being chosen for them by governments and corporations through censorship. Doctors and scientists are no longer free to express their own opinions. Despite years of training and research, I and many other physicians have been censored on social media simply for sharing our thoughts on how to live healthier lives. The Federal Trade Commission (FTC) even threatened to sue me for this, for a total of $1.2 million, in what should be a clear violation of my right to freedom of speech. My colleague, David Brownstein, MD, pursued legal action against the FTC for a similar letter. His lawyer requested a $20 million retainer and promised to take it all the way to the Supreme Court. Dr. Brownstein capitulated – he did not have $20 million to spare. If we are prohibited from fighting legal battles for our most fundamental rights, by the exorbitant costs of litigation, are we truly free to speak? I do not believe so. You would think that the right to freedom of speech would not require $20 million in litigation to settle. Sadly, corporations have bought the politicians, and politicians have appointed activist judges whose mental gymnastics make Simone Biles look like a quadraplegic.

Compare this state of affairs to the America of a hundred years ago. The average American grew, hunted, or fished much of their own food. They engaged in strenuous physical activity. They ate a local, seasonal diet. The government did not interfere with the cost of foods and the government did not interfere with speech about health and wellness. The government did not get to choose what healthcare it would pay for, and what healthcare it would allow citizens to offer or to obtain. Today, the government controls all of this and more about how Americans live, and therefore what it costs and what it

---

22   https://www.forbes.com/sites/chasewithorn/2021/04/06/nearly-500-people-have-become-billionaires-during-the-pandemic-year/?sh=101ce0ba25c0

takes to be healthy.

Slavery 2.0

I call this Slavery 2.0. In the old world, before the abolition of slavery, slaves knew that they were slaves. They were called slaves and they were treated as such. The doctrine of freedom that swept the world in the 1800's abolished the institution of slavery. Yet many modern people are little more than slaves. They believe what they are told and vote mindlessly for the same political party over and over again, despite obvious corruption and incompetence within those parties. They receive free television "programming," that constantly advances a socialist narrative and refuses to acknowledge the virtues of the alternative – freedom. They receive free healthcare, courtesy of the government. They receive free housing, thanks to government programs and subsidies. They receive food stamps to purchase food that is grossly unhealthy, the production of which is subsidized in the first place by taxpayer dollars. This enriches the three industries responsible for Slavery 2.0 – Big Food, Big Tech, and Big Pharma.

Slavery 2.0 has been the winning ticket in elections in the Western world since World War II. Yet for all the social programs, free stuff, and grandiose promises of politicians, the average American and European in 2021 is fatter, slower, dumber, more demented, uglier, and unhappier than their ancestors. They are not healthy, they are not wealthy, and they are not free. They are slaves to a global cabal of bankers, politicians, doctors, scientists, and bureaucrats who with each passing day treat them more and more like the slaves of the old world. I call this group of people totalitarian technocrats - people with a high degree of technical training and experience, who seek total control over society through technology. They wish to make freedom a memory, out of the conviction that they know better than everyone else how life should be lived.

"None are so hopelessly enslaved, as those who falsely believe they are free. The truth has been kept from the depth of their minds by masters who rule them with lies. They feed them on falsehoods till wrong looks like right in their eyes."

- Johann Wolfgang von Goethe

When it comes to health and healthcare, the government is stacking the deck against the average American. They seem determined to make it impossible to be healthy in this country. Health, it would seem, is meant to be a luxury that only the ultra-rich can afford. This is a sad state for a nation in which good health was taken for granted just a few generations ago.

It does not have to be this way. Americans deserve to be healthy, wealthy, and free. Anyone selling you less is just taking advantage of you.

While America sinks deeper into disease every day, much of the world remains a free, untamed place, where people still enjoy vigorous good health thanks to the stresses of everyday life. This should not surprise anyone—we are adapted to a world in which we must sustain a certain amount of environmental stress. When this stress builds our health, we call it "eustress." When present in excess, we call it "distress." People living close to nature—raising and hunting their own food, living in the fresh air, and drinking natural water have "eustress." People living in the modern world, behind computers, under artificial light, consuming processed foods and living under copious amounts of stress are in "distress."

This distress ultimately manifests as modern diseases that are seemingly incurable. They are not incurable. By changing what you eat, how you live, and how you think, you can reverse many modern, chronic diseases. This is a simple fact that Big Food, Big Tech, and Big Pharma do not want you to know, because if the whole world understood it, they would go bankrupt overnight.

Freedom Is Our Natural State

"The physician treats, but nature cures."

- Hippocrates

Why are people today so miserable and unhealthy? Modern technology has made them weak. They eat junk food, sleep during the day, stay up too late at night, abuse themselves in the gym, and rarely slow down to just relax. Diet and lifestyle changes can work wonders for the health problems of modern people. I have used this as the cornerstone of my practice and have been shocked by the results. Much of what I recommend to my patients is common sense, but it is too often overlooked in a world that has gone mad for drugs and surgeries, instead of simple solutions to complex problems.

This is not a new problem. There is nothing new under the sun, and this has been a problem since the dawn of civilization. We have all experienced this. Technology creates abundance, but within that abundance, we struggle to control our appetites. We become trapped by our lack of understanding of how small and seemingly inconsequential choices can have profound and devastating health consequences. A simple morning cigarette can lead to lung cancer. A simple cup of coffee can turn into a caffeine addiction, and a daily struggle with insomnia, headaches, and fatigue. A single line of cocaine turns into a lifetime of dissolute choices and regret. And yet, native peoples all over the world use addictive substances as part of daily life without significant health ramifications of any kind. Tobacco, coffee, and coca leaves are right now being used by people all over the world in a safe, controlled way that has no significant negative effect on their health.

This is the trouble with technology.[23,24,25,26,27,28,29] We use technology to create abundance, but abundance can create disease as surely as it can cure it. Technology can trap us in habits and choices that gradually undermine our health, until disease appears. The diseases we have come to know too well - obesity, diabetes, cancer, autoimmune diseases, allergies, cardiovascular disease, dementia, and mental illness – are all linked to the misuse of technology,,,,,,. These diseases together account for the overwhelming majority of premature morbidity and mortality in modern America. Many modern diseases are reversible. I have seen this with my own eyes, in case after case. We don't have to settle for a modern world where health escapes us, and disease deprives us of the happiness that is our birthright.

"Look deep into nature, and you will understand everything better."

- Albert Einstein

23   Rosen, L. D., et al. (2014). Media and technology use predicts ill-being among children, preteens and teenagers independent of the negative health impacts of exercise and eating habits. Computers in human behavior, 35, 364–375.
24   Rybnikova, N. A., Haim, A., & Portnov, B. A. (2016). Does artificial light-at-night exposure contribute to the worldwide obesity pandemic?. International journal of obesity (2005), 40(5), 815–823.
25   Reiter, R. J., et al. (2007). Light at night, chronodisruption, melatonin suppression, and cancer risk: a review. Critical reviews in oncogenesis, 13(4), 303–328.
26   Savitz, D. A., et al. (1999). Magnetic field exposure and cardiovascular disease mortality among electric utility workers. American journal of epidemiology, 149(2), 135–142.
27   Shandala, M. G., Dumanski⊠, U. D., Rudnev, M. I., Ershova, L. K., & Los, I. P. (1979). Study of non-ionizing microwave radiation effects upon the central nervous system and behavior reactions. Environmental health perspectives, 30, 115–121.
28   Johansson O. (2009). Disturbance of the immune system by electromagnetic fields-A potentially under-lying cause for cellular damage and tissue repair reduction which could lead to disease and impairment. Pathophysi-ology : the official journal of the International Society for Pathophysiology, 16(2-3), 157–177.
29   Gangi, S & Johansson, Olle. (2000). A theoretical model based upon mast cells and histamine to explain the recently proclaimed sensitivity to electric and/or magnetic fields in humans. Medical hypotheses. 54. 663-71.

These simple observations have led many people today to look into our past, to try to understand what made our ancestors so healthy. Thus, the "paleolithic" or "ancestral" health movements were born. I tell my patients that the short version of what I do is, "sell all of your worldly possessions and move to a tropical island." I am joking, of course, but this isn't that far from the truth. Yet no one has ever taken that advice. We are attached to the comforts and conveniences of our modern world. I am no exception to this rule, but I use modern technology and lead a modern life in a way that is compatible with my body's complex systems. That is the key to being healthy in our modern world.

People have struggled with this since the dawn of civilization. I am sure that shortly after our ancestors fashioned clay pots or rush baskets to store grain for lean times, they started to wonder how they could lose the extra weight that those stored grains could readily give them. This has led many people to adopt an extreme approach to health in which no modern amenities or foods are allowed—even "ancient" grains.

I do not believe the answer for our current health woes lies in abandoning grains, vilifying legumes, spending hours in ice baths or saunas, or sun-bathing until you look like a wrinkled paper-bag—just to name a few of the extreme practices that have arisen in recent years to fascinate and vex the public. I have found that we do not need to resort to these extremes to enjoy good health. On the contrary, I have found that any "healthy" practice can become injurious when taken to an extreme. Likewise, I have found our modern healthcare system — which always recommends more drugs, surgeries, and vaccines — to be an engine of disease creation and perpetuation, rather than resolution. They do not use the healing powers of nature, and so they fail to get their patients better.

"Physicians are many in title, but few in reality."

- Hippocrates

We are surrounded by supposed health experts, and yet the world has never been less healthy. We have never had such abundant resources with which to create health, and yet the world is struggling to contain epidemics of entirely preventable diseases. The answer from public health officials and doctors is, "give us more funding and power over your lives." This must be their idea of a sick joke, as these so-called "experts" have utterly failed to create health in a world where they have unprecedented power. To the contrary, their public health campaigns have in reality contributed to modern epidemics of disease, including the current "pandemic."

Of course we do not want to go back to a world without emergency medical services, running water, temperature control, and antibiotics. However, neither should we settle for a world in which, despite these amenities, our life expectancy is declining. We do not have to. In order to avoid this fate, we must pay close attention to how and why people are falling ill in our modern world. I spent two years of my career working in Northern Minnesota, on the borders of three different Native American reservations. I could easily see from photographs captured in the late 1800s, that just a few generations ago, these tribes had enjoyed remarkably good health. They had perfect teeth, skin, and strong bodies. They were free and they were healthy. This is not coincidence, it is causation. Then, their freedom was taken from them and they were herded onto reservations, where they were treated like slaves. Now, their descendants are struggling with some of the worst rates of diabetes, obesity, heart disease, dementia, depression, and substance abuse. Why?

The government restricted their liberties and then, to placate them, gave them free stuff. They receive free food, free healthcare, and free housing, and yet they are the sickest minority in the country. Wherever we go in our modern world, the more free stuff people receive, the sicker they are. I spent four years working as a traveling doctor and have practiced in Maine, New York, Minnesota, West Virginia, Virginia, Florida, Alabama, and Mississippi, and I can tell you that this is true from state to state and coast to coast.

"Free stuff" is poison. Yet the government can't seem to make enough of it to satisfy the petty wants of the public. The irony is that many people today seem to think that "free" healthcare is the solution to this problem. Nothing could be further from the truth. If you don't believe the example of the Native Americans, just ask a veteran or someone on Medicare. These people are not healthy, even if they have access to healthcare. Universal healthcare does not mean universal health—it means an endless supply of medical care that does not reverse modern diseases, but perpetuates them. Why? The pharmaceutical industry outspends every other industry in lobbying our government for special treatment. You can easily see how much money different politicians have taken from the pharmaceutical industry by going to OpenSecrets.org.

You will find that the elite of both dominant political parties are in the pockets of the pharmaceutical industry. You will also find that the industry tends to target outliers, who they label as radicals, for political destruction. Both radical progressives and radical conservatives end up on the hit list of the medical industrial complex, particularly if they propose legislation that will actually hurt the industry's bottom line. This is why political outsiders like Donald Trump, Tulsi Gabbard, Rand Paul, and Dennis Kucinich (just to name a few) are so viciously attacked by Beltway-insiders, who are probably better described as Beltway-sellouts or useful idiots. This is why our country is doomed if career politicians are not removed from office.

Freedom Is the Answer

The solution to these problems is not more government, which only serves the corporations that control it, but freedom. I was tempted to title this book 'Dying to Be Wild', but it isn't just a problem of "getting back to nature." The hippies did that, but they also ushered in an era of government overreach that has crippled the economy and yet failed to protect the consumer, the environment, and society in general. The problem is one of freedom. My patients today have the wealth necessary to pay me directly for my services, but they only have that wealth because the government hasn't taxed them into poverty yet. Many Americans have been taxed into poverty at this point. The tragic stories I hear on a regular basis of businesses being destroyed by the government are infuriating. I know that those families will struggle not only to pay for their healthcare, but to make the money they need to purchase what is essential to good health – healthy food and water, good air quality, and time to relax and rest, among other things. I know that many of those families will end up just like so many families in America's decaying cities and countryside – dependent upon the next government check. They do not need another check – they need their freedom back.

Good health is dependent upon freedom, but just because someone is free does not mean that they are healthy. While technology has given us an unprecedented level of freedom, it has also given us the means to destroy ourselves. This is why freedom is so easy to blame for the poor health of modern Americans. We have the means to create an endless buffet of unhealthy foods for unbelievably low prices. We can easily watch television or play video games all night. We can forget about drinking boring, unexciting water, and instead drink sweet tea, soda, or coffee. Technology is a double-edged sword that can improve our health or destroy it. It all depends on how we use it.

This has been a problem since the creation of the first simple machines.

Even simple machines give us the opportunity to over consume foods, to the point of excess. A dug-out canoe and a spear can lead a fisherman to eating only fish, just as an abundance of grain could lead a farmer to only eat grains. The first accounts of modern diseases are invariably linked to civilization – the ability to eat an imbalanced diet, divorced from the cycles of nature. Today, we don't just have the means to over consume certain foods. We can over consume everything. We can spend too much time indoors, we can spend too much time on technology, we can spend too much time sitting, lying down, running, or lifting weights. We are a nation of people struggling to find balance in our daily lives. Given the freedom to indulge in excess, some people will, even when it is obviously bad for them. This is human nature. This is why the impulse to deny people freedom has always been so tempting. Yet it always results in the abuse of power, in the service of accumulating more power. The challenge of technology is that it undermines human health insidiously, until health is a memory and the way back to it is a mystery.

Why do people abuse other people? There are many psychological phenomena and psychiatric diagnoses, but the ones that involve taking pleasure in harming others that I see most commonly are narcissism and psychopathy. These two related disorders explain why people desire to have power over others. I see this in my practice every day and it is all too common within healthcare workers themselves. Narcissists are far more common than psychopaths, and they are ruining American medicine. Narcissists are generally people who were abused and neglected as children. They lack empathy and actually take pleasure in the suffering of others. They feed off of the fears and anxieties of others. The healthcare field is a place where they can easily satisfy these desires. Doctors can manipulate patients into surgeries they do not need, hospital administrators can manipulate doctors into practices that do not serve or even harm patients, drug and device reps can manipulate doctors into prescribing medicines or using medical devices that are outright dangerous, and politicians can manipulate all of these people into doing whatever they want. When accused of malfeasance, these people engage in all of the classic tactics of narcissists to keep their victims enthralled and dependent upon the very system that is destroying them.

Good health means freedom, because only when we are at our healthiest can we be our most successful. Some people have never even known this kind of freedom. It is the freedom to go out and do something dangerous, just because you can, forsaking the comforts and safety of civilization for the risks and rewards of our natural state. Modern technology has created unprecedented levels of illness in our society, by drawing people away from nature and into unhealthy lifestyles, diets, environments, and mindsets. Public health experts would have us give up our liberties to rectify this situation, but they are incompetent at best and corrupt at worst. They do not understand how to create health out of disease. Rather than restrict people's liberties further, what is necessary to improve our health is to restore our liberties. People will ultimately make the right decisions and choose health over disease. Self-interest is our most fundamental drive, and our bodies are infinitely intelligent in their self-repair mechanisms.

In this book, I will explain how we got here, what is so wrong with the modern public health agenda, and give you insight as to how to ensure or even recover your good health. I will explain why liberty is synonymous with good health, and why the restriction of liberty inevitably leads to poor health and chronic disease. This is one of those books that the tyrants of the world want to make sure you do not read, let alone act upon.

We must begin by properly diagnosing what is truly destroying America's health and wealth – the parasitic trio of Big Food, Big Tech, and Big Pharma.

2. America's Parasites

How Big Pharma, Big Tech, and Big Food Are Destroying America's Health

"The physician treats, but nature cures."

- Hippocrates

Americans today are confronted by a paradoxical reality. How can we spend more money on our healthcare, publish more scientific studies, and develop new technologies and products every year, and yet have worse life expectancy and a rising cost of living?

There are three industries that are undermining the health and stealing the wealth of the average American (and citizens in most industrialized or post-industrial nations). They are Big Food, Big Tech, and Big Pharma. These three industries have used clever marketing to convince Americans to rely on fake food, fake medicine, and fake news, abandoning the healthy traditions of their ancestors. They have become parasites upon the American people, yet they are lauded as our leading industries. Americans are told to rejoice over the fact that these three enormous industries are only growing bigger. This "creates jobs." In reality, these three industries are destroying lives and lying about it on a grand scale.

What are fake food, fake news, and fake medicine? Fake food refers to the highly processed foods that Americans now rely upon for the sake of convenience and affordability. Fake medicine is healthcare that fails to restore or preserve good health, and in fact confers poor health due to over-treatment and over-diagnosis. Fake news provides the cover for fake medicine and fake food. The mainstream media have been carrying water for the food and pharmaceutical industries for years, because these are their largest advertisers. Fake news also includes things like social media, because so much of what people are exposed to via social media is pure misinformation.

To protect yourself from these three threats, you need to understand why these supposedly wonderful industries have turned to churning out poison.

Big Food

"Let thy food be thy medicine, and thy medicine be thy food."

- Hippocrates

After World War II, America's chemical industry turned from making bombs and ammunition to making fertilizer and pesticides. America had already experienced a revolution from the advent of pesticides almost a century earlier. The earliest pesticides were made with heavy metals like arsenic and lead. These were obviously toxic, but it took Americans decades to catch onto just how toxic they were. This is in part because many of America's drugs at the time were based on heavy metals like arsenic and mercury. Doctors had a financial incentive to portray their remedies as safe, not to mention effective, and were reluctant to label them as the poisons that they truly are.[30]

Pesticides and fertilizers together created record farm yields. This was called the "Green Revolution," for the remarkable increase in "greenery" that farmers were able to grow. However, as farmers continued to apply fertilizers and pesticides, they began to run into problems. Bugs, weeds, and fungi became resistant to pesticides. Plants were bred increasingly for productivity, rather than resilience, since farmers could just apply more pesticides if pests began to prey on crops. As plants and animals were increasingly overbred for productivity, they lost their natural resilience to disease. As bugs and pests became more resistant to pesticides, the crops themselves grew more vulnerable. The answer was not to pull back on breeding programs, but to increase the amount of pesticide use. Pesticide use has grown and grown, to the point that these dangerous chemicals are now detectable in many Americans.[31]

What has been the effect of increasing pesticide use? These chemicals are contributing to the rise of chronic disease in our nation. They are implicated in rising rates of cancer, autoimmune disease, allergies and asthma, and chronic neurological illnesses like autism and Alzheimer's disease.[32] Some of us have

---

30   Forrest Maready. "The Moth in the Iron Lung." 2018. Createspace Independent Publishing Platform. Page 65.
31   James S. Bus. (2015) Analysis of Moms Across America report suggesting bioaccumulation of glyphosate in U.S. mother's breast milk: Implausibility based on inconsistency with available body of glyphosate animal toxicokinetic, human biomonitoring, and physico-chemical data, Regulatory Toxicology and Pharmacology, 73(3), 758-764.
32   Seneff, S (2021) Toxic Legacy, Chelsea Green Publishing, Vermont USA.

concluded that DDT and other pesticides were the true cause of the polio epidemics that ravaged the nation during the mid-1900's.[33,34] What we are seeing today with COVID-19 has already played out with polio. The vaccines for polio, contrary to popular belief, were hardly effective. Furthermore, many people who died of polio did not in fact have polio virus isolated from their bodies. This is bad news for Big Pharma, which is one reason they are so vicious in silencing critics of the polio-virus myth. The pharmaceutical industry has made a fortune on polio vaccines since their initial release. The profits for Big Pharma and Big Food easily paid for an army of propagandists and experts who created the narrative that pesticides are harmless and vaccines are safe and effective. Yet success for Big Food came with a price. The Green Revolution was so successful that farmers over-produced food, to the point of impoverishing themselves by driving the price to record lows. The government implemented a program to support farmers – we now call these "farm subsidies." These subsidies are now some of the most destructive forces in America.

During this same period, refrigeration became widespread. My father, at 82, can clearly remember loading ice into an ice-chest in his boyhood home. He is the last generation that remembers a time before electrical refrigeration. The automobile and cold-storage revolutionized food storage and transportation. Suddenly, Americans were in a position to buy their food from hundreds of miles away, rather than right around the corner. A nation that had long been one of farmers who cooked and ate at home was on the verge of transforming into a nation hooked on fast food.

This combination of affordable food that could easily be transported over the nation's growing road system, combined with advances in mechanization and industrial production, set the stage for the mass-production of processed food. Food processing has always been with us, but it has made advances in the past few decades that dwarf those of past centuries and even millenia. Food processing was once an extremely laborious process. Food can now be hulled, husked, milled, blended, juiced, lyophilized, boiled, pasteurized, pressurized, or irradiated en masse. The result is that few people today start with single, raw ingredients to cook an entire meal. The American diet has been transformed from one of whole, fresh, local foods to one of fast, foreign, and preserved foods.

What is fake food? This is difficult to define. It is a catch-all term that I use for the sake of convenience. It is what happens when profits take precedence over quality. The consumer choosing between two brands of identical foods at

---

33   https://www.bmj.com/rapid-response/2011/10/30/ddt-must-be-bad
34   Suzanne Humphries, Roman Bystrianyk. "Dissolving Illusions." 2013. CreateSpace Independent Publishing Platform. Chapter 12.

the grocery store cannot know which is better without testing the foods. In the end, what differentiates real food from fake food is what has been added and what has been removed.

When food is processed, it is typical for its most vital nutrients to be removed. Heat and pressure can destroy vitamin C and many B-vitamins. Repeated freezing and thawing can as well. Removing husks, rinds, skins, or shells of food also changes their nutritional value. The "brown" portion of rice contains the B-vitamins that are necessary for the utilization of the carbohydrates (starches) within the rice. In nature, we frequently find that the micronutrients we need (vitamins and minerals) are present in quantities necessary to metabolize the macronutrients contained (fatty acids, proteins, and carbohydrates) within the same foods. Food processing often removes or destroys these vital nutrients, creating an imbalance between macro and micronutrients.

Many dangerous ingredients are added to processed foods. These include artificial flavorings, preservatives, colorings, and things like anti-humectants, anti-caking agents, anti-oxidants, and flavor enhancers. Many people are unwittingly sensitive to these additives. This is in addition to things added before the food is even picked. Pesticides, herbicides, fungicides, and heavy metals now contaminate our food. Many patients are unwittingly being poisoned by these food additives.

As fake food has taken over the American diet, diseases linked to food have rapidly increased in prevalence and severity. There is no simple, easy way to define "fake food." There is also no clear line across which one passes from a "harmless" amount to a "harmful" amount. Details matter, and this is why I spend hours discussing diet with each and every patient. The bottom line is that this general trend in the consumption of processed, over-bred food has led to a deterioration in the health of the public. The government is actively enabling and encouraging this destruction of our public health.

Today, Big Food is bigger than ever. A handful of grocery stores provide the bulk of what Americans eat. A handful of food manufacturers produce the products that occupy 99% of America's grocery store shelves. Meanwhile, the farmers who got rich from the Green Revolution have been betrayed by these corporations. Farmer suicides continue to rise and farm bankruptcies peaked in 2020.[35] America's small family farms are dying out.

How did Big Food get so big? They lobbied the government for special

---

35   https://www.forbes.com/sites/niallmccarthy/2020/02/10/us-farm-bankruptcies-reach-eight-year-high-infographic/

protections, subsidies, and privileges. This problem has become so blatant and outrageous that Barack Obama passed a bill that has been nicknamed the, "Monsanto Protection Act."[36] Why does one of the largest corporations in history need the government to pass an act protecting it? They obviously do not need this kind of protection. The whole premise of the Constitution is that all Americans are afforded the same protections and privileges under the law. Clearly, we no longer live in a Constitutional Republic. We live in a Socialist Republic, where some corporations and individuals enjoy more privileges than others. Tom Vilsack was named Secretary of Agriculture (2008-2017) of the United States Department of Agriculture. He is the former Vice President of Monsanto. He was later reinstated in 2021 by Joe Biden. Monsanto has better representation within our government than the everyday American.

Many Americans are more afraid of COVID-19 than they are of processed food. I find this ironic, since virtually everyone who has died or been disabled by COVID-19 has suffered from diseases and underlying conditions that are caused by eating processed food (or they have been extremely old).[37]

If Americans would vote to enact sensible agricultural reforms, to create a food system where everyone ate healthy, wholesome food, COVID-19 would never have been more than a bad weekend in a few intensive care units. Instead, it is being used as an opportunity to deprive us of what little liberty we have left.

Big Food relies upon over-breeding and pesticides to create cheap products, but creating these products is only the first step on their path to profitability. They needed to get Americans to buy their products, and that means advertising. Advertising today, and since the invention of the radio, has been in the hands of a few people within a single industry. These people have shaped the way we view our world. Today, this industry is known as Big Tech.

Big Tech

"He who controls the present controls the past."

- George Orwell

---

36   https://www.centerforfoodsafety.org/press-releases/3961/the-monsanto-protection-act-is-back-and-worse-than-ever

37   Al-Sabah, S., Al-Haddad, M., Al-Youha, S., Jamal, M., & Almazeedi, S. (2020). COVID-19: Impact of obesity and diabetes on disease severity. Clinical Obesity, 10(6), e12414.

Big Tech is generally meant to refer to large technology firms, like Google, Facebook, Twitter, Microsoft, and Apple. This is a narrow definition of Big Tech. Mainstream media outlets are hardly "Big Tech," but their news is increasingly disseminated and consumed through software and hardware that are. Virtually all news today is consumed via technologies invented in the last few decades. I define Big Tech as the major technologies that have emerged in the past few decades – radio, the internet, wireless networks, smart devices, laptops, tablets, and the software that power them. These technologies are all interconnected, and anyone doing business today is, by extension, beholden to Big Tech companies to purvey their information and products to the public. This leaves them at the mercy of Big Tech. Big Tech exerts enormous influence over the media in particular, because media outlets know that their reach can be destroyed by changes to proprietary algorithms, or they can simply be deleted from the app store or dumped from their web-hosting services.

Big Tech depends upon two key technologies to give their customers what they want. The first of these is visible light. Advances in screen technology now allow you to watch anything you want, virtually anywhere. The second is microwave and radiowave radiation. These frequencies allow our tech devices to transmit information wirelessly. Visible light from screens and invisible microwave and radiowave emissions are what I refer to as fake light. Each has negative health effects that are carefully being concealed by the industries that depend upon them for their profits. This is done in part by the corruption of scientific inquiry. Those who study these phenomena live in constant fear of losing their jobs and tarnishing their reputations. Professor Olle Johannsson is just one such researcher who, despite continually doing groundbreaking and insightful research, was "evicted" from his lab in the world famous Karolinska Institutet in Sweden in an attempt to silence his work.[38] Even when experts like Dr. Johannsson speak out, the mainstream media ignores or denigrates their work.

Both of these technologies have been shown to be hazardous to human health. The question is to what degree and in what dose. This has become one of the most controversial questions in modern public health. The first wireless device was the radio, invented in the early 1900's by Guglielmo Marconi. He died an early death, perhaps because of over-exposure to radio and microwaves. The first electronic screens emerged after World War II. The four-inch screen that my mother watched Howdy-Doody on had become twenty inch screens by the time I was a boy. Now, television screens are frequently eighty inches or more. The amount of light being emitted is many times what it was just a generation ago. Meanwhile, the amount of wireless radiation being emitted by

---

38   https://www.magdahavas.com/wp-content/uploads/2011/06/Weigel-2011.pdf

household and personal devices has increased by many orders of magnitude. The cell phone in your pocket emits more microwave radiation in a day than your grandparents might have encountered in an entire lifetime.

As these exposures have increased, the health of many Americans has deteriorated rapidly. Many experts dismiss the dangers of modern technology, because it is difficult to impossible to study them in isolation. For example, if you want to study the effects of cell phone radiation on brain cancer, how do you do it? The best studies are from Scandinavian brain cancer registries, which capture virtually all malignant brain tumors in their highly stable population. However, even then, there are many confounding variables that go uncontrolled. For example, in the time we have gone from simple flip phones to smart phones, we have also invented wireless headphones and earpieces, smart watches, and home wireless networks. Each of these devices emits a variable amount of radio or microwave radiation. How can you control for this? Those of us who actually measure, test, and mitigate these factors have seen astonishing improvements in our patient's health that defy modern epidemiological methods to adequately capture. This means that it is easy for the industry to fund studies that fail to find associations between disease and technology. This playbook was originally written by the tobacco companies, but it is being perfected by Big Tech, Big Food, and Big Pharma. Research done in the Soviet Union so clearly demonstrated this[39] that to this day, Russia and Eastern European countries have radically different safety standards for levels of electromagnetic radiation in the environment.[40] Western scientists, on the other hand, have been busy enriching themselves with industry funding, and have failed to do the kind of research that Soviet scientists did decades ago. The technology industry is constantly funding new research to cast doubt upon the clear and present danger of wireless radiation.

While the dangers of microwave and radiowave emissions are hotly debated, the hazards of excessive blue and green light, especially at night, are widely accepted.[41] What makes light so dangerous? The light that modern screens and light bulbs emit is unlike anything ever before seen on earth. In 2007, the World Health Organization[42] listed shift work as a risk factor for cancer. Most people have no idea that this announcement ever took place. Millions of people are working evening or night jobs without any knowledge of how hazardous it is to their long-term health. This advisory came after decades of research among night shift workers revealed significant increases in their risk

39   https://avaate.org/IMG/pdf/mcree80_rev_soviet.pdf
40   https://www.emfs.info/limits/world/
41   Hatori, M., Gronfier, C., Van Gelder, R.N. et al. (2017) Global rise of potential health hazards caused by blue light-induced circadian disruption in modern aging societies. npj Aging Mech Dis 3, 9.
42   https://www.esmo.org/oncology-news/Night-Shift-Work-Classified-as-Probably-Carcinogenic-to-Humans

of cancer. To this day, public health authorities do little, if anything, to help people understand the negative health effects of fake light.

The health hazards of technology extend far beyond their physical interactions with your body. Technology can radically change your relationship with your environment, and this has health consequences. A hundred years ago, the average child spent much of their time outside. Even in cold, harsh winters, children had nothing to do indoors except read. The outdoors was their escape. Now, I see toddlers and young children playing with tablets and smartphones – their electronic babysitters. We have no idea how this will change our children. It is a vast experiment in how light interacts with biology. The average American spends approximately 95% of their time indoors. They rarely see the sun. They stay up late at night, bathing in fake light that keeps them awake, and then they wonder why they are suffering from anxiety, depression, or insomnia.[43] They wonder why they develop cancers[44] and heart disease[45] earlier than their parents.

Big Tech's bottom line depends upon keeping the public in the dark (pun intended) regarding the dangers of their devices. To those of us who counsel our patients to put down their devices and spend time in nature, it is obvious that modern technology is a significant health hazard. I now frankly tell patients that if they cannot alter their technology use, they may never get the results that they want. Big Tech censors doctors like me, who dare to tell the truth about the dangers of their products.[46] Their influence over elections ensures that our government is dominated by politicians who protect their interests. The 1996 Telecommunications Act grants immunity to the telecommunications industry from health effects caused by their products, specifically wireless technologies. Why would they need immunity if their products were safe?[47]

This is why Big Tech is so eager to de-platform doctors like me. They seek to cast us into a kind of internet purgatory, as they did to my friend Laura Loomer. This is why, if you appreciate my candid and in-depth content, you should subscribe to my telegram channel (t.me/stillmanmd) and substack (stillmanmd.substack.com).

Big Tech is actively destroying the public's health. Their media platforms

---

43   Kardaras, Nicholas. Glow kids: How screen addiction is hijacking our kids-and how to break the trance. St. Martin's Press, 2016.
44   Hubbard, A. K., Spector, L. G., Fortuna, G., Marcotte, E. L., & Poynter, J. N. (2019). Trends in international incidence of pediatric cancers in children under 5 years of age: 1988–2012. JNCI cancer spectrum, 3(1), pkz007.
45   https://health.clevelandclinic.org/why-are-heart-attacks-on-the-rise-in-young-people/
46   https://twitter.com/martinkulldorff/status/1317768803862839301?lang=en
47   https://ehtrust.org/policy/the-telecommunications-act-of-1996/

are the marketing vehicle for Big Food and for the last of the parasitic industries that is destroying our republic – Big Pharma.

Big Pharma

"I firmly believe that if the whole materia medica as now used could be sunk to the bottom of the sea, it would be all the better for mankind-and all the worse for the fishes."

- Oliver Wendell Holmes

Big Pharma could be better called, "Big Healthcare." Big Pharma, however, essentially controls all of healthcare. They have gradually been taking over the industry since the early 1900's. In 1911, Abraham Flexner published the "Flexner Report." This report detailed the quality of different medical schools in the United States. Several schools closed as a result of the report. Those that remained began to focus increasingly on pharmaceuticals as medicine. Meanwhile, advances in chemistry allowed scientists to manufacture or isolate chemicals with greater and greater precision. Herbalists were replaced by druggists, or pharmacists. Penicillin was discovered shortly after World War I, starting a new chapter in the history of medicine. Doctors could suddenly treat overwhelming infections with a few grams of white powder.

Drugs became increasingly popular and increasingly profitable. Drug companies became larger and larger. However, drug companies have an incentive to sell products, rather than to see that patients remain well or recover from illness. Drug companies began to encourage doctors to prescribe more and more of their drugs. These drugs, or the means to produce them, were patented. They were far more profitable than other forms of medicine. Doctors were easily bribed and manipulated. Drugs came to dominate modern medicine, complemented by surgery. Surgery was a quick, grisly affair prior to the invention of modern surgical devices, antibiotics, and sedatives. Modern medicine is, for the most part, founded on pharmaceuticals.

Today, the drug companies control all aspects of medicine, albeit indirectly. They are almost twice as profitable as similarly sized corporations in other industries. They are some of the largest contributors to political parties in the United States. This is not a partisan issue. Both Republicans and Democrats take money from the pharmaceutical industry. This would explain why so little meaningful legislative action is taken to make drugs more affordable, or to reduce the need for them. This is why health insurance premiums, including for Medicare, rise year after year. Why is it that your cell phone gets better, bigger, and faster as it gets more expensive, but your health and your healthcare get worse? The answer is that the drug companies control healthcare and are shamelessly parasitizing the American people.

How do drug companies control medicine? They have the money to fund political campaigns, and therefore control politicians. They buy virtually all of the advertising in medical journals, which derive the bulk of their income from these ads. Drug companies account for a large proportion of advertising revenue for television and other forms of media. They can therefore exert enormous control over these companies. This is one reason why so much news coverage of the pharmaceutical industry is either covering up for industry malfeasance, or outright selling drugs to the public.

What about insurance companies? Health insurance is one of the greatest scams in history. The industry operates as a cartel. You cannot simply open a health insurance company, you must seek approval from the state insurance boards. There are also extremely onerous laws regarding how health insurance companies operate. Chief among these is that health insurance should be tied to employment. This law serves no positive purpose but to make the business of health insurance more complex and convoluted, so as to discourage competition. Big Pharma makes sure that health insurance companies reimburse doctors in such a way that doctors prescribe more drugs – by making visits short, so that no education can take place as to how to prevent or reverse disease. I rarely prescribe drugs – I might only prescribe a few times a month. This is because I may spend an hour with each patient in a single visit, and I help them to reverse their illnesses. I am delivering the kind of healthcare that people actually value and will pay for, but health insurance companies will not pay me for this level of service. I do not enrich the pharmaceutical companies, hospitals, other doctors, or medical laboratories. This makes me an outsider to modern medicine, yet how I operate is the solution to our healthcare crisis. This is why drug companies have taken such pains to control politics. It is through politics that they are waging economic warfare on physicians who practice good medicine, while rewarding those who only prescribe drugs.

This has been going on for over a hundred years. Chiropractors in the 1800's fought a long and bitter legal battle with medical doctors for their right to practice. Many of them endured jail and fines, but refused to give up. Still, the drug companies have managed to marginalize chiropractic, as well as virtually all other non-pharmaceutical healing modalities. These modalities are a threat to Big Pharma's profit model – their goal is to maximize prescriptions.

The reality is that the vast majority of drugs prescribed today treat diseases that are preventable. Big Pharma wages a relentless propaganda war on the public to convince them there is nothing they can do about their diseases. They do this by controlling government research, academic research, and medical publishing. The pharmaceutical industry can make or break a physician or scientist's career. If they fund your research, let alone hand you clinical trials to publish, then they can rapidly build your resume of citations. In the modern academic world, physicians are judged not by the quality or impact of their research, but by the volume of their research. The more papers they have their name on, the more influential they become. Many of these physicians find their way to institutions like the National Institutes of Health, which controls government funding of medical research. This is not wild speculation. This is the opinion of some of medicine's leading editors and researchers. Marcia Angell former editor of the New England Journal of Medicine, wrote about this in her book, "The Truth About the Drug Companies."[48] Richard Smith, former editor of the British Medical Journal, wrote about it in his book, "The Problem with Medical Journals." Many other whistleblowers have come forward to go on the record about how conflicts of interest in medicine are shaping a narrative in which drugs and surgeries cure, and nothing else is even worth publishing about.

I left academic medicine in disgust after seeing firsthand how pointless such a career would be. When you serve industry and publish meaningless studies, you climb the academic ladder. You do not have time to help patients, only to prescribe to them. You do not change lives, you merely change medications. This is not medicine – it is a disgrace. Hippocrates wrote long ago that, "The greatest medicine of all is teaching people how not to need it." This should be standard practice in medicine. Instead, it is a forgotten ideal.

Big Pharma has hijacked modern medicine. Over the past century, it has run it aground. American medicine, and by extension medicine all over the world, has fallen prey to the greed of Big Pharma. Doctors today are as much indoctrinated as they are educated as to how to treat, let alone cure, disease. They are trained to practice in such a way that the system (hospitals, insurance companies, pharmaceutical companies, and medical device manufacturers) makes the most money possible. They are blind to their indoctrination. They do not think they are susceptible to clever marketing disguised as "science." This is why many of my patients are experts within the health and wellness field, including other doctors, drug company executives, and drug and device sales people. They realize that clever marketing has ruined medicine. Fortunately,

---

48   Angell. M 2005, The Truth About the Drug Companies: How They Deceive Us and What to Do About It

there are still those of us practicing to a higher standard than those set by the pharmaceutical company marketing teams. Our goal is to free our patients from prescriptions, diseases, office visits, medical bills, and high insurance premiums – so that they can get on with life.

How Big Food, Big Tech, and Big Pharma Are Destroying America

Big Food creates diseases that are treated by the drugs made by Big Pharma. Big Tech provides cover and advertising space for both. Together, they collude with one another to silence opposition and maintain the status quo. They control much of our politics, because they shape the narratives around some of our most basic needs as human beings – food, medical care, and interaction with others. They are lying to us to shape a narrative that maximizes their profits, at the expense of the health and wealth of us all. This is why I do not shrink from calling them parasites. They are criminal enterprises, and the true extent of their criminality is just barely visible to the public.

Where are the regulators? If tomorrow, America's public health experts decided to actually do something about the problems posed by Big Tech, Big Food, and Big Pharma, they could end the healthcare crisis practically overnight. If tomorrow, the heads of the National Institutes of Health, the Food and Drug Administration, the United States Department of Agriculture, and the Centers for Disease Control told people to vote only for candidates who would enact legislation to provide healthy, wholesome food for all Americans, it could be done. Instead, they go to work covering for these parasitic industries, and studiously ignore the root of America's public health problems. This is because they are making money working for those industries, or expect to one day work for those industries. The American public health establishment has been completely corrupted by the very people they are supposed to protect us from. The rats are guarding the cheese. The foxes are guarding the henhouse.

How did we get to this point? This struggle between those of us who want to be free, and those who want to deny us our liberties is not new. The struggle for the health of society is as old as society itself. This is not a modern problem, it is a perpetual one. There is truly nothing new under the sun. All of this has happened before, and all of it will probably happen again.

"We learn from history that we do not learn from history."

- Hegel

Those who live in ignorance of medical history are prone to fall for the clever marketing gimmicks of doctors, hospitals, and pharmaceutical companies. History shows clearly that as bright as doctors are, they are not bright enough to avoid being fooled en masse. We are just witnessing the latest episode of this.

To understand our current circumstances, you have to understand the dangers of playing doctor.

3. The Dangers of Playing Doctor

Why Playing Doctor Is One of the Most Dangerous Things You Can Do

"The reason doctors are so dangerous is that they believe in what they are doing."

- Robert S. Mendelsohn, MD

Spending money on your health is one of the most dangerous things you can do. If this surprises you, consider the following.

Did you know that 50% of stents used to open clogged arteries to the heart are unnecessary?[49] Of those stents that are placed, a certain percentage will cause complications, such as stroke, heart attack, or even death. Cardiologists are too zealous about stenting, because they get paid to do it (though they do see life-saving benefits in emergency cases).[50]

Still, that is small consolation for those who do not actually need a stent and suffer a stroke, heart attack, or even death as a complication of receiving one.

People tend to fall for all kinds of gimmicks, frauds, and simplistic thinking. I know this all too well—the world of medicine is largely hucksters selling drugs, supplements, surgeries, and gadgets to people indiscriminately. Why is this? First, if something can be a medicine, then it can be a poison. This leads many people to experience relief with various "therapies," but others will feel and perform worse with the same therapy. Second, doctors and patients both want to be right and hate to be wrong. This creates what we call the placebo effect. Doctors have a long history of fooling themselves into

49   Devi, Sharmila. "US physicians urge end to unnecessary stent operations." The Lancet 378.9792 (2011): 651-652.
50   Boden, William E. "Mounting Evidence for Lack of PCI Benefit in Stable Ischemic Heart Disease: What More Will It Take to Turn the Tide of Treatment?: Comment on Initial Coronary Stent Implantation With Medical Therapy vs Medical Therapy Alone for Stable Coronary Artery Disease." Archives of internal medicine 172.4 (2012): 319-321.

believing what they are doing is of benefit to the patient, and fooling patients into agreeing with them. The word 'doctor' is derived from the word 'docere', meaning to teach. Unfortunately, this noble profession has morphed out of its original meaning towards something that closely resembles a dictator. Most people have a strong tendency to blindly believe their doctors because of the surrounding prestige. Instead, patients should be demanding that doctors first and foremost teach their patients how to get well and stay well. Now we are in a time where one cannot question the authoritative position of a doctor; this is unless that doctor is outside of the mainstream view that is carefully and deliberately choreographed by Big Pharma, Big Tech and Big Food. The moment they question their narrative, they become a quack.

Because living beings are complex systems, it is very difficult to isolate therapies that work reliably, or are worth the adverse effects and risks. Yet people believe that "experts" are more often right than wrong. This is absurd when you look at the actual track record of experts.[51] What is perhaps more perverse than the arrogance of experts is the arrogance of those who continue to follow them, even after their advice has proven flawed.

Take bloodletting as one example. Bloodletting (more properly known as therapeutic phlebotomy) is the practice of cutting open a patient and allowing them to bleed. Technically, drawing blood for labs is bloodletting. So is blood donation. So is cutting your finger with a knife while cooking dinner. Not long ago, doctors widely agreed that bloodletting had therapeutic value. George Washington was famously bled of many pints of blood before he finally succumbed to pneumonia (although he may well have died of blood loss).

The practice has, in modern years, been vilified as hopelessly backward and foolish. After all, the notion that you could make a patient better by literally injuring them is counter-intuitive, to say the least. However, that is exactly what any elective and many emergency surgical procedures do. The question is, how do you know when to cut and when not to cut? The history of surgery is littered with examples of surgical procedures that sound good in theory, but fail to benefit the patients in practice (that is why we call it "practicing" medicine). Likewise, many surgeries began as grisly experiments, including surgeries we still perform today. The first five mitral valve commissurotomy patients all died post-operatively. The surgeon who innovated the procedure was nicknamed, "Bailey the Butcher." His sixth patient, however, made a full recovery and lived a full life.[52] He saved her life. If he had stopped at five, who knows where the world of open heart surgery would be today? What seems like butchery may be

---

51   Taleb, Nassim Nicholas. Incerto 4-Book Bundle: Fooled by Randomness, The Black Swan, The Bed of Procrustes, Antifragile. Random House, 2016.
52   Zalaquett, S. R. (2009). Sixty years of mitral valve surgery. Revista medica de Chile, 137(9), 1253-1260.

the antecedent to a life-saving surgery.

Bloodletting must have seemed wrong-headed from the start. Why then did doctors gravitate toward the practice of bloodletting? First, it is something that doctors can do. Doctors love to "do" things. "Don't just stand there, do something!" This simple phrase illustrates one of the greatest fallacies that people tend to fall for—that doing something is better than doing nothing. Few patients have the wisdom to know when to pay their doctors to do nothing. Those who think that they are only getting better when they are paying the doctor to "do something" are bound to waste an extraordinary amount of time and money, and they may risk their lives in the futile effort to get a bargain.

"Sometimes to do nothing is a good remedy."

- Hippocrates

The father of medicine, thousands of years ago, warned us against overly aggressive practitioners of medicine. They always have and always will be with us. Still, while it is easy to deride bloodletting as quackery, we must ask: "When is bloodletting of therapeutic value?" There are times when it is appropriate, so the question becomes who, when, where, and how much?

The Benefits of Blood-Letting

What is blood? Can you have too much of it? If the answer is yes, then it follows that you could benefit from bloodletting. Blood contains plasma and red blood cells. Plasma contains proteins and red blood cells contain hemoglobin. The blood carries protein around the body, where it is used to nourish your organs and tissues. The hemoglobin in the red blood cells contains iron, and this carries oxygen to your cells to be burned to create energy, and carries carbon dioxide away to be exhaled.

Could you have too much protein or too many red blood cells? The answer is yes. Patients who have a type of arthritis known as gout have a tendency to have too much protein in their blood. A study in 2003 found that, "During a 28-month follow-up, maintenance of NID was found to be safe and beneficial in all patients, with effects ranging from a complete remission to a marked reduction of incidence and severity of gouty attacks."[53] What this study means is that donating blood might relieve gout patients of their severe, crippling pain - regardless of other medication or lifestyle factors. Patients with a disease known as polycythemia vera have too many blood cells, and patients with hemochromatosis, which results in iron-overload, need to give blood in order to keep their iron levels down. Blood donation is necessary for good health in these cases. The idea that blood-letting is quackery is an over-simplification. Bloodletting has a place.

This is confirmed in clinical practice. Many patients who fit this profile do feel better after giving blood. This is also not just my opinion based on anecdotal evidence—major clinical studies have found this benefit. The Kuopio Ischaemic Heart Disease Risk Factor Study found that, "blood donors had a 88% reduced risk (relative hazard = 0.12, 95% confidence interval 0.02–0.86, p = 0.035) of acute myocardial infarction, compared with non-blood donors."[54] In the Copenhagen City Heart Study, "The death rate increased from 10 to 15% (depending on cause of death) for every 100-point increase in ferritin."[55]

Dr. Dennis Mangan wrote an entire book on the health benefits of blood donation, called, "Dumping Iron."[56] Toxicologist, Jym Moon, PhD wrote a similar book, "Iron: The Most Toxic Element."[57] These books document the literature supporting the use of phlebotomy in iron-overloaded patients.

Why might donating blood confer a therapeutic benefit?

Iron is not only a nutrient, it is a potential toxin. Patients who have mutations in a gene known as the HFE gene tend to accumulate too much iron. They develop diabetes, arthritis, dementia, heart disease, liver failure, and low sex hormone levels (for starters) at a very early age as a result.

Sound familiar? These diseases account for a substantial amount of the healthcare spending in the modern world today. Yes, iron is a nutrient, but you truly can have too much of a good thing.

When does iron become toxic? When it has accumulated to levels that the body cannot control. Your body needs copper, vitamin A, and multiple

53   Facchini, F. S. (2003). Near-iron deficiency-induced remission of gouty arthritis. Rheumatology, 42(12), 1550-1555.
54   Salonen, J. T., Tuomainen, T. P., Salonen, R., Lakka, T. A., & Nyyssonen, K. (1998). Donation of blood is associated with reduced risk of myocardial infarction: the Kuopio Ischaemic Heart Disease Risk Factor Study. American journal of epidemiology, 148(5), 445-451.
55   Ellervik, Christina, Jacob Louis Marott, Anne Tybjærg-Hansen, Peter Schnohr, and Børge G. Nord-estgaard. "Total and cause-specific mortality by moderately and markedly increased ferritin concentrations: general population study and meta analysis." Clinical chemistry 60, no. 11 (2014): 1419-1428.
56   Mangan, P.D (2016) Dumping Iron: How to Ditch This Secret Killer and Reclaim Your Health
57   Moon, Jym. Iron: the most toxic metal. George Ohsawa Macrobiotic, 2008.

B vitamins to control iron[58,59,60,61]. When it lacks these micronutrients, iron accumulates in cells and cannot get out into the bloodstream. When this happens, patients may look like they have iron deficiency anemia. In fact, they may just have low vitamin A or low copper levels. This is not due to a total-body iron deficit, but an inability of the body to move iron out of cells. Hormonal imbalances can cause the same issue.[62]

Why might people today have too much iron?

We are losing less and less of it, and eating more and more of it. Our bodies have no way to excrete iron. We lose very little each day. We easily exceed our losses with common foods, even with moderate intake. Flours are now fortified with iron, which now constitutes a substantial proportion of our iron intake. This is frankly dangerous to members of the public who have HFE gene mutations that predispose to iron overload. This mutation is so common in individuals of Northern European ancestry that Sweden stopped fortifying its food with iron in 1995, citing the public health risks.

Women can control their menstrual cycles with hormonal birth control. Every cycle they miss is extra iron they are accumulating. Dr. Jerome Sullivan proposed that it is menstruation that explains why women have a lower rate of heart attacks than men until menopause.[63] After menopause, they catch up rapidly. Women also formerly lost enormous amounts of iron in childbirth. Thanks to emergency medical services, we now stop bleeding very quickly and efficiently. We may presume that not long ago, when our ancestors engaged in incessant tribal warfare, men must have lost blood in battle. Last, but not least, parasites love to feed on blood. Hookworms, mosquitoes, and ticks are just a few of the parasites that feed on human blood. Malaria was once common as far north as Denmark[64], and hookworms were so prevalent in the American south after the Civil War that they represented a public health crisis.[65]

We used to lose a lot more blood than we do now, and we used to

58   Fishman, S. M., Christian, P., & West, K. P. (2000). The role of vitamins in the prevention and control of anaemia. Public health nutrition, 3(2), 125–150.
59   Semba, R. D., & Bloem, M. W. (2002). The anemia of vitamin A deficiency: epidemiology and pathogenesis. European journal of clinical nutrition, 56(4), 271–281.
60   Michelazzo, F. B., Oliveira, J. M., Stefanello, J., Luzia, L. A., & Rondó, P. H. (2013). The influence of vitamin A supplementation on iron status. Nutrients, 5(11), 4399–4413.
61   Smith, E. M., & Tangpricha, V. (2015). Vitamin D and anemia: insights into an emerging association. Current opinion in endocrinology, diabetes, and obesity, 22(6), 432–438.
62   Kautz, L., Jung, G., Valore, E. V., Rivella, S., Nemeth, E., & Ganz, T. (2014). Identification of erythroferrone as an erythroid regulator of iron metabolism. Nature genetics, 46(7), 678–684.
63   Sullivan J. L. (1981). Iron and the sex difference in heart disease risk. Lancet (London, England), 1(8233), 1293–1294.
64   https://en.ssi.dk/surveillance-and-preparedness/surveillance-in-denmark/annual-reports-on-disease-incidence/malaria-2018
65   Brinkley, G. (1997). The Decline in Southern Agricultural Output, 1860–1880. The Journal of Economic History, 57(1), 116-138.

consume a lot less iron. There can be no doubt that we are, as a society, accumulating more and more iron. This is having untold negative health consequences.

And yet, if you know anything about iron and health, it is probably this.

Iron is a nutrient, without which you would die. Bleeding is bad for you, and silly doctors in times past who didn't know any better, thought it was a good idea to drain the body of "extra" or "bad" blood.

"Foolish the doctor who despises the knowledge acquired by the ancients."

- Hippocrates

We are conceited enough to think that we know better than our ancestors did, without pausing to reflect upon why they may have thought what they thought. Despite an abundance of evidence to the contrary, we like to think that we know just what to do, and that our approach to life needs little correction. One of the great physicians of American history, Sir William Osler, said to a graduating medical school class, "Gentlemen, half of what we have taught you is in error. The problem is that we do not know which half."

Bloodletting has therapeutic value. It can also be dangerous. The devil is in how much, how often, and under what circumstances one should recommend it.

Bloodletting is just one of many examples I could share with you from the pages of medical history of a therapy that has value, but that has fallen by the wayside and is now denigrated as a quaint and unscientific practice.

It is remarkable to see how modern people ignore wisdom of prior generations, to abandon potentially valuable therapeutics. We like to think of progress, in medicine and science in general, as inevitable. But if we are capable of forgetting what works and embracing what does not, then how do we ensure continued medical and scientific progress? The answer, of course, is freedom. To deceive people into embracing bad medicine and rejecting good medicine, the first thing you have to do is control the narrative by corrupting those who author it. In this case, that means doctors.

The Corruption of Medicine and Our Misplaced Faith in Vaccines

"It is difficult to get a man to understand something, when his salary depends on his not understanding it."

- Upton Sinclair

Doctors are people too. People have a tendency to rationalize what will make them more money. Doctors are no different. The pharmaceutical industry has known this for years, and is adept at manipulating doctors into practicing medicine in a way that maximizes Big Pharma profits. Many insiders have written about corruption in medicine and science. "The Truth About the Drug Companies," by Marcia Angel and "The Trouble with Medical Journals," by Richard Smith are memoirs of two highly accomplished editors of medical journals, in which they explain in detail how Big Pharma has compromised medical journals. Marcia Angel is the former editor for the New England Journal of Medicine. and Richard Smith is the former editor of the British Medical Journal. These are two of the most prestigious medical journals in the world. Their editors have openly denounced the current academic process as corrupt and unreliable. Why should anyone consider science "settled" when some of its greatest minds consider its fundamental process—peer-review and publication—to be seriously flawed?

In 2014, a CDC insider named Dr. William Thompson contacted autism researcher Brian Hooker about a cover-up at the CDC regarding the relationship between autism and vaccines. Hooker recorded four phone calls with Thompson, in which Thompson admitted that the CDC had covered up data. Thompson never officially went public, but the transcripts that Hooker obtained are damning evidence of corruption at the CDC.[66] People like Robert F. Kennedy Jr. have spent their lives fighting corruption at the CDC and FDA surrounding vaccines. He documented this most recently in his book, "The Real Anthony Fauci." We have the proof. Why do people still trust these institutions? The short answer is that the media ignores these stories and continues to consider these institutions the "gold standard." This is nonsense.

There have been exposes from within Big Pharma itself. John Virapenen was a manager at Eli Lilly who wrote a memoir of Big Pharma corruption shortly before he died. He details the bribing of physicians with cash payments

---

66   Barry, K. (2015). Vaccine Whistleblower: exposing autism research fraud at the CDC. Simon and Schuster.

and research grants. He explains how research trials are faked and then the cooked data is submitted to the FDA, which often approves the drugs without ever investigating the reliability of the data. One scandal after another confirms what skeptics and whistleblowers say about Big Pharma – they have rigged the game in their favor and they don't care how many people die because of their malfeasance.

This is why an increasing proportion of the public is skeptical of doctors. They have always been skeptical of doctors, and they always should be. Ironically, one of the most popular medical interventions today, vaccination, has a dubious past. Vaccination originally was performed by doctors using a variety of needles and bladed instruments that they would use to inoculate the skin of the patient with whatever they wanted to induce immunity against. Just imagine: if someone walked up to you on the street corner waving a scalpel covered in the purulent discharges of another human being or animal, promising you that it would provide you with immunity to an illness, you would think them insane, right? Yet that is what doctors did. There can be no doubt that some patients must have died of vaccination, so crude were its methods and so limited were the means of modern medicine at the time to treat infections.

Yet the practice has become so popular that people now regard it with a zeal comparable to the religious fervor of the Middle Ages, when heretics were burnt at the stake. Despite this fervor, vaccination is not—and never will be—harmless. My practice is full of patients who have been harmed by vaccines. What can be a medicine can also be a poison. The question is rather whether their purported benefits outweigh their risks. By its supporters, we are directed to the endless number of studies supporting the safety of vaccines and deriding concerns over safety. On the other hand, we have industry insiders, who know how these studies are performed, vetted, and then published, telling us we cannot trust the journals publishing them. In addition to the vaccine-injured, I have also attracted patients who work in clinical research, pharmaceutical sales, and medical device sales. They laugh when I ask them what they think of "science" today. Every area of so-called scientific medicine is riddled with junk science. Scientists and doctors can be bought, data can then be manufactured or scrubbed, and statistics can be manipulated to justify virtually any conclusion regarding diagnosis and treatment. This problem is so rampant that it led John Ioannidis, MD, PhD, to author an article entitled, "Why Most Published Research Findings Are False."[67] He was derided by academics, but he is also one of the most widely published and well respected physicians alive today. He

---

[67]   Ioannidis, John PA. "Why most published research findings are false." PLoS medicine 2, no. 8 (2005): e124.

did not write that fateful paper lightly, as such controversial opinions have a way of getting academics exiled from academia.

Vaccination has become a sacred cow in our society—you are not allowed to question it. I have never regarded it as such. My mother always told me that my allergies and ear infections had started right after a round of infant vaccinations. My sister's eyes crossed and she subsequently developed sinusitis just after a round of vaccines. We cannot prove causation in either case, but, then again, how does one prove causation when it comes to vaccines? My sister eventually required surgery to restore normal vision and another surgery to relieve her sinusitis. This was when my mother jumped ship on conventional medicine, to see what "alternative" medicine had to offer. My father, on the other hand, insisted we be vaccinated. I distinctly remember being held down by my father and a nurse, to be forcibly injected with vaccines as a child.

I received all of my childhood vaccines, on schedule, and I received all vaccinations recommended until approximately one year ago. I had my doubts about vaccination from the start, but hoped that I was wrong. I accepted what I was told in medical school—that vaccines are safe and effective, and that they saved us from horrors of past infectious diseases.

I was invited to question the sacred cow of vaccination during medical school by Thomas Platts-Mills, MD, PhD. I spent a lot of time in Platts-Mills's lab during medical school. He was one of the foremost scientists at the University of Virginia at that time. He was one of a small number of people to have a publication in the revered New England Journal of Medicine. He was the former president of the American Academy of Asthma, Allergy, and Immunology. He had been knighted by the queen for his contributions to the field of allergy. He was the only allergist to have achieved that honor. Tom had impeccable credentials and an unimpeachable academic record.

He asked me one day, "Why do we give newborns the hepatitis B vaccine?" Hepatitis B is a virus that affects the liver, and is spread by sexual contact or injection drug use. Do we think that parents are going to go home and sexually abuse their children or inject them with drugs? If not, then do we assume that the parents are infected and may pass it somehow to their children? In that case, why not just test the parents for hepatitis B and, if they are negative, not vaccinate the child? Tom pointed out to me that newborns do not make antibodies. When we test adults for immunity to hepatitis B, we do it by testing their antibody levels. If newborns do not make antibodies, then why are we immunizing them with a vaccine that we then judge based upon an antibody test?

45

Tom plainly thought that something was wrong with this policy, but he never said so publicly. That would have been catastrophic for his career, despite the influence and clout that he had gained over decades in academia. I believe this is why, during 2020 and 2021, so few immunologists and virologists have come forward to challenge the narratives that have been used to justify lockdowns and forced vaccination.

In the late summer and early fall of 2021, I went undercover with Project Veritas to see what I could find out about the COVID-19 vaccines. As part of that investigation, I read extensively on the history and science of vaccination. I spoke to industry insiders and colleagues. I read opinions by both those who support vaccination, and those who oppose it, and everyone in between. I directly interviewed subject matter experts. My investigations left no doubt in my mind that vaccines cause more harm than good as they are currently employed.

This is exactly the opposite of what I was taught in medical school, where I was taught that vaccines are highly effective at preventing infection with and transmission of viruses and bacteria. Vaccines are therefore chiefly responsible for delivering us from the horrific infant mortality of antiquity and the industrial revolution. They are practically harmless and always effective, even when administered in large numbers simultaneously. The scientific data supporting their use is sound and unquestionable. The few people who do question these assertions are dangerous quacks who must be ignored. They are preying upon the impressionable in order to sell more snake oil to enrich themselves.

I pose the following questions to you, in the context of facts that you can easily confirm from publicly available sources.

First, how well do vaccines prevent infection with and transmission of viral and bacterial disease? The father of vaccination, William Jenner, published a paper in 1798 claiming his vaccination technique provided lifelong immunity to smallpox. Doctors of the time immediately challenged and proved his assertion wrong by copying his methods and then observing smallpox infection in those who had been vaccinated.[68] Smallpox mortality remained essentially unchanged following vaccination campaigns, even when the vaccines were mandated.[69] Likewise, those who had been vaccinated against smallpox were not reliably protected. There are few exact figures on the morbidity and mortality among those who had been vaccinated, but the first smallpox vaccination was

---

68 Suzanne Humphreys MD and Roman Bystrianyk, Dissolving Illusions: Diseases, Vaccines, and the Forgotten History (CreateSpace Publishing, 2017). Page 70.

69 Suzanne Humphreys MD and Roman Bystrianyk, Dissolving Illusions: Diseases, Vaccines, and the Forgotten History (CreateSpace Publishing, 2017). Pages 93-94.

far from a resounding success.

Smallpox and most other infectious diseases declined regardless of vaccination in the late 1800s and early 1900s, thanks to improved sanitation, nutrition, and environmental quality.[70]

I would argue that it was one of the worst frauds ever perpetrated upon the world by doctors. Smallpox was not eradicated by a vaccine. It was eradicated by improvements in public sanitation, air quality, nutrition, and personal hygiene.

What about polio? Generations of Americans have been raised to believe that polio was a vicious paralytic disease afflicting children that was eradicated thanks to a vaccine. If that is the case, then why did we only see epidemics of polio arise in the late 1800's and early 1900's? Why were they not reported previously? The prevalence of polio has never been very high. And the word "polio" is too vague to be meaningful. Poliomyelitis is reported to be an illness in which polio virus ascends from its usual home in the gastrointestinal tract to destroy components of the spinal cord, causing the dreaded paralysis. If the disease continues to ascend the nervous system, it will reach the brain, potentially proving lethal. Any of a variety of viruses can do this. These viruses are all strikingly similar. The clinical presentation of this disease is identical to many other flaccid paralyses, many of which are not caused by viruses.

If polio is a disease that must be banished with vaccination, then why don't populations that avoid vaccination, such as the Amish or Christian Scientists, struggle with epidemics of paralytic polio? In fact, studies of isolated native tribes have clearly documented that these populations harbor polio viruses, and that they have natural herd immunity. There is a lack of documented paralytic polio among them. Some will say that this is just because there are so few of them, but there are thousands and thousands of people in the United States who do not vaccinate, and yet we do not see news reports of epidemics of polio within these populations. Experts are quick to tell us that these people are just protected thanks to herd immunity—that the vaccinated are insulating them from viruses that would surely strike them down if not for vaccination. If that is the case, then why do native tribes all harbor these viruses? There is probably not a single human being on planet earth who does not harbor more than one virus in their gut that has been documented to cause paralysis. Yet where are the cases of paralysis due to these viruses?[71]

70   Suzanne Humphreys MD and Roman Bystrianyk, Dissolving Illusions: Diseases, Vaccines, and the Forgotten History (CreateSpace Publishing, 2017). Pages 196-201.
71   Suzanne Humphreys MD and Roman Bystrianyk, Dissolving Illusions: Diseases, Vaccines, and the Forgotten History (CreateSpace Publishing, 2017). Page 228.

Dr. Albert Sabin, inventor of the oral polio vaccine, asked the following question in 1947:

"... the most important question: why did paralytic poliomyelitis become an epidemic disease only a little more than fifty years ago, and as such why does it seem to be affecting more and more the countries in which sanitation and hygiene, along with the general standard of living, are presumably making the greatest advances, while other large parts of the world, regardless of latitude, are still relatively unaffected?" [72]

In the fifty years prior to his writing, the radio, electricity, the lightbulb, the telephone, penicillin, pesticides, and chemical warfare had all been discovered. The world was awash in new physical and chemical forces, each of which we now know to affect living organisms in complex and diverse ways.

I pose a similar question to you today. Why are neurological and psychiatric diseases becoming epidemics today, and why are they more and more affecting countries in which sanitation and hygiene, along with the general standard of living, are presumably making the greatest advances, while other large parts of the world, regardless of latitude, are still relatively unaffected?

What percentage of "polio" was and is due to the actual polio virus? In the 1958 Michigan polio epidemic, fecal samples were obtained from 869 patients. Almost half had no detectable virus in their stool. Only 292 had evidence of polio virus. Another 100 had evidence of Echo virus, and another 73 had evidence of Coxsackievirus. How, exactly, could this be called a "polio" epidemic? Of the 191 patients who had blood samples taken, 123 showed no antibody change to any virus. Only forty-eight showed a rise in antibody levels to polio virus, another fourteen to Echo, and another six to Coxsackie. [73]

What, exactly, is the disease we once called "poliomyelitis?"

My mother had polio. She distinctly recalls being unable to walk. She has severe neck pain that she attributes to polio to this day. Yet we have no idea what actually caused her illness. Today, more than a thousand cases of a disease called transverse myelitis are diagnosed in the United States each year. This disease is reported to frequently follow vaccination. Officially, it is considered "idiopathic," which means that doctors cannot agree on a single cause or combination of causal factors. This disease can look exactly like poliomyelitis.

I find the notion that vaccines have delivered us from the horrors

72   Albert B. Sabin MD, "The Epidemiology of Poliomyelitis: Problems at Home and Among the Armed Forces Abroad," Journal of the American Medical Association, vol. 134 (June 28, 1947): 749-756.
73   Brown, Gordon C., Willard R. Lenz, and George H. Agate. "Laboratory data on the Detroit poliomyelitis epidemic—1958." Journal of the American Medical Association 172.8 (1960): 807-812.

of infectious disease to be laughable. Microbes cause disease sporadically, and most severely in the malnourished, chronically ill, and elderly. They are opportunistic and rarely cause disability or death in healthy, happy people. Those cases of "healthy" people succumbing to, for example, COVID-19, are either extremely rare or pure fabrication. I know from the extensive lab testing that I perform in my practice that the majority of Americans are malnourished in some way, or indulge in bad habits that are destroying their health, often without even knowing it. There are few people in our country who are truly "healthy."

The evidence supporting vaccination does not meet the gold standard we would hold any other therapy to – a randomized, placebo-controlled clinical trial. When scientists and physicians have undertaken these studies, they have found increased rates and severity of chronic diseases in their vaccinated patients – just as I have found in taking care of families that formerly vaccinated their children. The scientific consensus for vaccination is based on pure pharmaceutical industry propaganda, promoted by doctors whose livelihoods depend upon vaccination.

"Torture the data long enough, and they will confess anything."

- Ronald Coase

Did vaccines deliver us from the horrors of high infant mortality in the late 1800s and early 1900s? The data is quite clear that most of the reduction in mortality took place in the late 1800s, and that it had nothing to do with the primitive vaccination methods of the time.

Second, regardless of their historical track-record, are modern vaccines effective? Outbreaks routinely occur among those previously vaccinated. The unvaccinated frequently escape infection, let alone death. How effective are vaccines at reducing infection by and transmission of diseases? Why should we care in cases of mild diseases like chicken pox or measles? Diseases such as these are here today and gone within a week, and those who are properly nourished stand a negligible chance of death or disability from these diseases.

If the purpose of a medicine is to prolong life and prevent death, then why do we care about rates of infection and transmission anyway? How should we judge vaccine efficacy? The current "gold standard" in vaccinology is to judge them by their ability to provoke a humoral immune response. Yet having a humoral immune response does not imply that one is actually immune, because antibodies can actually backfire and make your reaction to an illness worse, a phenomenon called antibody-dependent enhancement.[74] This is far from a wild theory. It has derailed past vaccine-development projects. It may well be at work right now with modern COVID-19 vaccines.

In 2019, the United States Food and Drug Administration granted restricted approval to a Sanofi Pasteur against the viral hemorrhagic fever called dengue. Dengue is a mosquito-borne illness. The reason that only limited approval was given is that the vaccine sensitized some recipients to more severe dengue.[75] How does this happen? When we inject a foreign substance into the body, the body makes antibodies (proteins that try to destroy the foreign protein) against it. Yet not all antibodies are equal. Some are more effective than others, and some are outright dangerous. If, for example, someone makes immunoglobulin type E to something as innocuous as bee or ant venom, it may cause an overwhelming allergic reaction called anaphylaxis. This can lead to death. In overwhelming infections, it is in fact the immune system that often kills the patient. This is why in many instances, we find that providing steroids that suppress the immune system leads to improved survival. This is why certain vaccines may provoke dangerous immune responses in certain patients. In such cases, it would be more apt to call the vaccine a poison rather than a medicine. This is what is meant by antibody-dependent enhancement.

Dengue vaccine development began in the 1920's. Even if the 2019 vaccine is safe and effective, dengue is an example of 100 years of vaccine failure.[76] Should we be so bold as to presume that we can do in months for one virus what was not done in a century for another? Is the current dengue vaccine even safe? How many people must be vaccinated to save one life? These are questions that remain open to debate.

If the primary purpose of vaccination is to reduce morbidity and mortality associated with infectious diseases, why don't we judge vaccine efficacy based on reductions in total mortality and disability of the vaccinated compared to the unvaccinated? The gold-standard in studying a therapeutic such as vaccination should be metrics such as hospitalizations, deaths, and healthcare expenditures per number of study subjects. In other words, how many hospitalizations, deaths, emergency room visits, doctor's visits, prescriptions,

74   Arvin, Ann M., Katja Fink, Michael A. Schmid, Andrea Cathcart, Roberto Spreafico, Colin Havenar-Daughton, Antonio Lanzavecchia, Davide Corti, and Herbert W. Virgin. "A perspective on potential antibody-dependent enhancement of SARS-CoV-2." Nature 584, no. 7821 (2020): 353-363.
75   Shukla, Rahul, Viswanathan Ramasamy, Rajgokul K. Shanmugam, Richa Ahuja, and Navin Khanna. "Antibody-dependent enhancement: A challenge for developing a safe dengue vaccine." Frontiers in Cellular and Infection Microbiology 10 (2020).
76   McArthur, Monica A., Marcelo B. Sztein, and Robert Edelman. "Dengue vaccines: recent developments, ongoing challenges and current candidates." Expert review of vaccines 12, no. 8 (2013): 933-953.

days absent from school or work, and so on, do we see in the vaccinated versus the unvaccinated?

No one performs studies like this. They are considered unnecessary. Why? What could be more important work, scientifically, than documenting the tremendous benefits of vaccination with such conclusive and incontrovertible studies? There are plenty of populations who would volunteer for the control group of such an experiment: Christian Scientists, the Amish, the Hutterites, religious conservatives of all faiths, and the remarkable proportion of the population who attribute their and their families disabilities to vaccines - the so-called "anti-vaxxers." Twenty three percent of those resisting COVID-19 vaccination have PhDs.[77,78] So much for being "anti-science."

Where does the data for vaccination come from? First, it comes from trials that are designed, performed, and paid for by the pharmaceutical industry. The problems with this are astounding and are best described in the book, "The Illusion of Evidence-Based Medicine".[79] Second, the data comes from large-scale government databases, created and maintained by government employees, who have incestuous relationships with the industry that they control. The pharmaceutical industry has repeatedly been convicted of fraud over the past several decades. They have knowingly and repeatedly endangered the lives of countless people, causing incalculable harm. Why would anyone assume them to be completely innocent in this case?

Third, are vaccines safe? How can we even begin to assess this question when the industry that makes them is routinely engaged in criminal activity, and their regulators are drawn from the ranks of the industry itself? How can we evaluate this based on data from clinical trials that is not available to the public? The pharmaceutical industry owns the data it generates – the public has no right to see it. Much of it remains unavailable for scrutiny. Who knows what we would find if all drug trial data was mandated to be made public?

We might start by asking, "are pharmaceutical companies being adequately punished for their crimes?" The short answer is no. A 2018 report by Public Citizen (citizen.org) reported the following:

"Financial penalties continued to pale in comparison to company profits, with the $38.6 billion in penalties from 1991 through 2017 amounting to only 5% of the $711 billion in net profits made by the 11 largest global drug companies during just 10 of those 27 years (2003-2012).[80]

77   https://unherd.com/thepost/the-most-vaccine-hesitant-education-group-of-all-phds/
78   https://www.medrxiv.org/content/10.1101/2021.07.20.21260795v1.full.pdf
79   Jureidini, J, McHenry, L (2021), The Illusion of Evidence-Based Medicine
80   Page 6 (https://www.citizen.org/wp-content/uploads/2408.pdf)

Why would the pharmaceutical industry be honest, when being dishonest is so profitable? We can be sure that the pharmaceutical industry is getting away with much more than they are being prosecuted for in the judicial system. What is the true extent of the harm they have done to innocent people?

Why, then, should anyone trust their products?

Compare buying a vaccine to buying a car. Cars are safe and effective, yet they are also dangerous. Would you buy a car from a company that had routinely lied about the safety of its product? That had knowingly endangered its customers? Would you trust their safety data? Would you trust the government inspectors who approved their product, and vouched for the validity of the data that supports its safety? Why would you?

If tomorrow a major car company were convicted of criminal activity and it became known that thousands or even millions of their customers had died unnecessarily, what would happen? Under what circumstances would you purchase a car from that company? Yet we are told to trust the pharmaceutical industry to be truthful with us about one of its most profitable product lines. Is it so unreasonable to be skeptical of this situation? Even more disgusting, the government mandates that children receive these vaccines to attend school. They mandate that soldiers receive them to fight in our armed forces. Yet there is no reason to believe the safety data behind these vaccines.

Vaccines are in fact so dangerous that drug companies only continue to manufacture them because they are no longer liable for their harms. In the 1980s, vaccine manufacturers lost so many lawsuits over vaccine-damaged children, that they threatened to stop making vaccines. In the wake of their legal losses in the 1980s, Congress passed the "National Vaccine Compensation Act."[81] This bill established a vaccine injury court and exempted vaccine manufacturers of all liability for their products. Today, an excise tax is made on all vaccines. This tax is paid by patients and insurance companies when they purchase vaccines from doctors.

In other words, the money spent by consumers and insurance companies on vaccines is in part funding the injuries caused by those vaccines. If vaccines are safe and effective, then why do they require a special tax to pay for the harms that they cause?

Imagine if someone were to run for office on a platform of exempting oil companies, automobile manufacturers, gun or ammunition makers, or home-builders from liability for their products. Prices might plummet for these

81   https://www.hrsa.gov/vaccine-compensation/about/index.html

goods, but so would quality. When companies have no liability for dangers of their products, they worry less about the dangers and allow consumers to assume the risk. Smart consumers look at such products as insane gambles, and avoid them even if the risk is small. If you talk to people about products they love and trust, you quickly realize that one of the first things people look for is reliability. Reliability is built by constantly improving upon the product, as with subsequent iterations you improve performance and quality and reduce risks and defects.

Not so with vaccines. Every year, every car maker makes a new model of every single one of their cars. They are safer, faster, stronger, more fuel efficient, and yet they are sometimes even cheaper than the previous year's model. Why is this not the case with vaccines? We have created an industry with perverse incentives, where innovation is not rewarded, where liability is assumed by the public, and where profits are taken by the cartel we call the pharmaceutical industry.

Fourth, what if vaccines cause long-term health damage? Vaccines alter our immune systems. They contain toxic adjuvants like aluminum and, until recently, mercury. It is a well-established principle of toxicology that small exposures over long periods of time, without acute poisoning, can still lead to long term health consequences. Smoking just a few cigarettes a day is still unhealthy, even if it's only a few.

My beliefs on this topic were shaped by those of my mentor, Dr. Platts-Mills. Dr. Platts-Mills's skepticism about vaccination was founded on decades of research and experience as a physician. One of the central topics of his research was that excessive hygiene was responsible for much of the allergic, autoimmune, and other chronic diseases of the modern world. He knew that children living a more rural, agrarian life, free of pollution and, coincidentally, modern medical care, suffered from a lower rate and severity of allergic and autoimmune diseases.

Why might this be the case? The short answer is that too much hygiene is unhealthy. This research began in the 1980s in Germany, when researchers made the surprising discovery that children raised in homes with wood-burning stoves had a lower likelihood of developing asthma, eczema, and other allergic diseases. They had expected the air pollution from wood-burning stoves to have the opposite effect—to increase allergic diseases.[82] What they had not anticipated was that these children tended to live on dairy farms. They might spend the day in a bassinet in the barn, where their parents were busy tending

---

82   von Mutius, Erika. "The "Hygiene Hypothesis" and the Lessons Learnt From Farm Studies." Frontiers in Immunology 12 (2021): 808.

the cows. They grew up spending time outdoors, consuming a largely local and seasonal diet.

Researchers then studied this in the Amish in the United States.[83] The Amish follow the same way of life that they have since they arrived in the United States over a hundred years ago, and they use little technology. The findings of the German researchers were quickly confirmed in study after study. There is such a thing as being too clean. This has become known as "The Hygiene Hypothesis." Yet we cannot simply blame hygiene for these differences. With differences in hygiene, we see differences in many other factors. The children on these farms are not just exposed to more of nature (including bacteria, viruses, fungi, and parasites) than their more urban peers. They are exposed to less industrial and urban air pollution. They tend to drink well water rather than municipal water. They tend to play outside more. They tend to get less medical care, due to the remote nature of their homes. They are exposed to lower levels of radiofrequency and microwave radiation from cell phones and radar. They tend to have fewer gadgets that keep them up all night. They tend to watch less television. They tend to receive fewer vaccinations. There are so many variables to account for that the question becomes academic. In short, modernization has brought with it many modern plagues, that modern medicine is impotent to cure.

The practical question is simply, "how should we live?" We now have decades of research on the hygiene hypothesis and on the human microbiome, and the answer is clearly that lack of exposure to our natural environment is a health hazard. If there is such a thing as being "too clean," then is there such a thing as being "too vaccinated?" Have we made a tragic error in trying to innovate our way around illnesses like chicken pox and even polio?

This begs another question. What is our optimal relationship with bacteria, viruses, fungi, and parasites? If the studies on "The Hygiene Hypothesis" are any indication, then we require a certain amount of "infection" to avoid immunological diseases like allergies. Yet modern physicians and researchers have little interest in asking, let alone answering, this question. I am sure that for many of them, doing so would be fatal to their careers. Physicians such as myself wonder if we will be allowed to continue practicing medicine just for voicing these concerns.

There is ample literature supporting the premise that infection is a healthy part of life. Why might this be? One of the hallmarks of infection is a

83   Stein, Michelle M., Cara L. Hrusch, Justyna Gozdz, Catherine Igartua, Vadim Pivniouk, Sean E. Murray, Julie G. Ledford et al. "Innate immunity and asthma risk in Amish and Hutterite farm children." New England journal of medicine 375, no. 5 (2016): 411-421.

fever. Fevers activate the immune system and have long been recognized as a source of healing.

"Give me the power to create a fever, and I shall cure any disease."

- Parmenides

Fever is one of the body's main defenses against infection. Many infectious agents do not operate well at higher temperatures. Even a degree or two difference can make a substantial impact on their viability. When the body mounts a fever, it increases blood flow to the inflamed area. The immune system - immunoglobulins and white blood cells - is brought to the area by the blood. Fever protects us from melanoma.[84] Metastatic, malignant melanoma has been reported cured following repeated fevers.[85] This is not a single, isolated case. The history of medicine is full of stories of cancer remission after the induction of fever.[86] There is even evidence to suggest that, as infectious diseases have declined in incidence, cancer incidence has risen.[87] Cancer is now the second leading cause of death in America. Have we merely traded one cause of death for another? Does the answer to the cancer epidemic perhaps lie in fever therapy? Why does modern oncology ignore fever therapy? Perhaps it has to do with the profit margins of chemotherapy, which are much larger than those of fever therapy.

Infections seem to educate and improve our immune systems. We seem to be best served by a certain amount of infection, rather than complete eradication. This improved or "better educated" immune system may then be more effective at seeking out and destroying cancer cells.

Could vaccination be contributing to the increasing rates of certain types of cancer that we are seeing today? If infections protect us from cancer, thanks to how they augment and modulate our immune responses, then would suppressing infections lead to increased cancer incidence and severity?

If viruses have been with us since the beginning of time, might they

84   Kölmel, K. F., A. Pfahlberg, G. Mastrangelo, M. Niin, I. N. Botev, C. Seebacher, D. Schneider et al. "Infections and melanoma risk: results of a multicentre EORTC case-control study. European Organization for Research and Treatment of Cancer." Melanoma Research 9, no. 5 (1999): 511-519.
85   Wrotek, Sylwia, Łukasz Brycht, Weronika Wrotek, and Wiesław Kozak. "Fever as a factor contributing to long-term survival in a patient with metastatic melanoma: A case report." Complementary therapies in medicine 38 (2018): 7-10.
86   Hobohm, Uwe. "Fever therapy revisited." British Journal of Cancer 92.3 (2005): 421-425.
87   Kleef, Ralf, Wayne B. Jonas, Wolfgang Knogler, and Werner Stenzinger. "Fever, cancer incidence and spontaneous remissions." Neuroimmunomodulation 9, no. 2 (2001): 55-64.

not play some important role in the maturation of our immune systems? We know that children in more modern societies (who tend to have received more vaccines) have more allergies, autoimmune diseases, neurological and psychiatric issues than children living in less modern nations. The idea that vaccination is changing our immune systems, and our health in general, for the worse is far from a conspiracy theory. It is only considered a fringe idea because physicians and scientists are afraid of losing their position and their income for questioning it. Thomas Cowan, MD, wrote about this in his book, "Vaccines, Autoimmunity, and the Changing Nature of Childhood Illness."[88]

The Truth About the COVID-19 Vaccines

"No one is more hated than he who speaks the truth."

- Plato

When I first began working on this book, we were told that vaccines were the answer to COVID-19. Since then, numerous breakthrough infections have been documented in those who have received the vaccines. The protection that was reported at first was always debatable, and has steadily waned with time. As of December 6th, 2021, nearly 20,000 deaths[89] have been reported to the Vaccine Adverse Events Reporting System regarding the COVID-19 injections.[90] Deaths are reported to this system when they have occurred shortly after receiving a vaccine. This number dwarfs the number of vaccine deaths reports in past years. If all other vaccines are still being administered at the same rate, then this would imply that the COVID-19 vaccine is causing more deaths than all over vaccines combined.[91]

If COVID-19 vaccines do not completely protect us from COVID-19, and the vaccines are more deadly than all over vaccines combined, then who is to say that the vaccine is preferable to the disease?

---

88   Cowan, Thomas. Vaccines, Autoimmunity, and the Changing Nature of Childhood Illness. Chelsea Green Publishing, 2018.
89   United States Department of Health and Human Services (DHHS), Public Health Service (PHS), Centers for Disease Control (CDC) / Food and Drug Administration (FDA), Vaccine Adverse Event Reporting System (VAERS) 1990 - 11/26/2021, CDC WONDER On-line Database. Accessed at http://wonder.cdc.gov/vaers.html on Dec 3, 2021 9:04:00 PM
90   https://openvaers.com/
91   United States Department of Health and Human Services (DHHS), Public Health Service (PHS), Centers for Disease Control (CDC) / Food and Drug Administration (FDA), Vaccine Adverse Event Reporting System (VAERS) 1990 - 11/26/2021, CDC WONDER On-line Database. Accessed at http://wonder.cdc.gov/vaers.html on Dec 3, 2021 9:02:46 PM

The real question we should be asking is, does the COVID-19 vaccine reduce your risk of death? This is how therapeutics should be studied, because this is how therapeutics are delivered in the real-world. Academics instead want us to blindly accept pharmaceutical company data, generated over months, rather than years. The people who are telling you that the vaccines are safe and effective know this based on mere months of data. Vaccines usually go through two years of study before approval. The COVID-19 vaccine went through just six months of study.

The tens of thousands of deaths reported to the VAERS database are just the beginning. Far, far more complications will inevitably be reported in the years to come. For many, this is the last vaccine they will ever take, due to the severity of the side effects. The public health establishment has successfully alienated millions of Americans, who may never trust another vaccine again. Rather than ensuring the safety and efficacy of the products they are now forcing on the public, they are censoring doctors and scientists who have reasonable and valid concerns about these vaccines.

Expert after expert, from doctors to virologists to epidemiologists, have come forward to counter the mainstream narrative that the COVID-19 vaccines are safe and effective. They have written entire books and held conferences on the topic. Drs. Robert Malone[92], Peter McCullough, Paule Elias, Scott Atlas, Richard Urso, Ryan Cole, Pierre Kory, and Paul Mari[93]k lead the list of doctors who have been fighting the false narrative that the vaccine is safe, let alone safer than ivermectin.[94]

Excellent reporting has been done elsewhere as to the conflicts of interest between the public health establishment, academic medicine, and the pharmaceutical industry. I do not have time to cover them here. John Virapen, a former drug company executive, wrote about bribing officials and rigging trials in his memoir, "Side Effects: Death." Mary Holland, Kim Rosenberg, and Eileen Iorio wrote about problems with the HPV vaccine in, "The HPV Vaccine on Trial." Carl Elliott wrote about corruption in medical research in, "White Coat Black Hat." I have accumulated a small library on the topic at this point, and yet people like me are labeled as conspiracy theorists.

Meanwhile, the fear mongering continues. Cooler heads continue to avoid the vaccine.

---

92   https://rwmalonemd.substack.com/
93   https://covid19criticalcare.com/
94   https://brownstone.org/

"The welfare of humanity is always the alibi of tyrants."

- Albert Camu

Those of us who question the orthodoxy of vaccination have everything to lose and little to gain. We can be heroes to a minority of the population who avoid vaccines, but we stand to lose everything we have professionally. Doctors and scientists can be fired. Researchers can lose their funding. Doctors (and any healthcare practitioner) can lose their licenses, and therefore their livelihoods. Despite this, our concern is so sincere and well-founded that we cannot but come forward to speak the truth. Independent physicians, scientists, lawyers, and activists like Robert F. Kennedy Jr., Judy Mikovits, Andrew Wakefield, Mary Holland, Kim Rosenberg, Kent Hickenlively, Brian Hooker, Del Bigtree, Paul Thomas, Thomas Cowan, Suzanne Humphries, and Roman Bystrianyk - to name a very small number - have all published scathing indictments of vaccine science and vaccine policy.

Why is vaccination so popular, while bloodletting has fallen into such disrepute?

Bloodletting and vaccination differ in one important regard. Vaccination entails patentable medications that can be sold over and over again to a public that will persistently need them, as their immunity wanes. This makes vaccination extremely profitable. Pfizer has made $36 billion[95] in 2021 from its COVID-19 vaccine. This does not include the rise in the price of Pfizer stock. Bloodletting is something people do for charity. It will never make anyone a fortune.

These dark truths of human nature are found in the pages of our history from the beginning of time.

You may not like it, but the simple fact is that much of what passes for "evidence-based medicine" today is pure nonsense, fabricated by industries that are minting fortunes off of the reputation of "science." Your doctor is just as gullible as you are, and therefore may be the worst person to get your medical advice from.

This has always been the case. It is not just a modern problem. Yet it is the central problem of what we call "civilization." As bad ideas accumulate in the popular consciousness as "true," despite all evidence to the contrary,

---

95   https://reliefweb.int/report/world/pfizer-biontech-and-moderna-making-1000-profit-every-second-while-world-s-poorest

civilizations gradually decay and eventually fall.

"A new scientific truth does not triumph by convincing its opponents and making them see the light, but rather because its opponents eventually die and a new generation grows up that is familiar with it. . . . An important scientific innovation rarely makes its way by gradually winning over and converting its opponents: it rarely happens that Saul becomes Paul. What does happen is that its opponents gradually die out, and that the growing generation is familiarized with the ideas from the beginning: another instance of the fact that the future lies with the youth."

- Max Planck

How significant is this problem? How gullible are people, really? I have just told you that people are foolish enough to be duped en masse, and that they will attack those who disagree with them, no matter how obviously right they are. I have told you that the best and brightest in any society are apt to fall into erroneous thinking, until ultimately their civilizations crumble around them. Even as their civilizations are crumbling, they persist in their delusions.

How does this happen? How do ideas that are demonstrably false take root in the popular consciousness? And what can we do to identify them?

The answer lies in how we perceive reality. We can easily be trapped by our own misperceptions, or, as Tesla put it, "deficient observation." Understanding this is the first step in avoiding the traps of modern life, which lead to premature disease and death.

4. Misinformation Masquerading as Marketing

How Corporations Addict You to Bad Decisions

"Deficient observation is merely a form of ignorance and responsible for the many morbid notions and foolish ideas prevailing."

- Nikola Tesla

We have the most advanced sense organs on the planet. I do not mean that we have the sharpest vision, the most sensitive fingertips, the keenest hearing, or the most delicate senses of smell and taste, but in aggregate, we (arguably) have a broader range of senses and a more sophisticated means of interpreting them than any other animal on earth. We can see more colors, perceive more sounds, taste more flavors, and, more importantly, we have an extremely large brain that can integrate these senses to "make sense" of the world around us. Other animals have sharper vision, better hearing, or a heightened sense of smell, and uncanny means of sensing everything from rotting flesh (vultures and other carrion animals) to fresh blood (sharks), but they cannot interpret these sensations and manipulate our surroundings the way we can.

Animals use cues from their environments to make decisions. Bears choose when to hibernate based on how long the sun is out and how cold it is. Grazing animals like caribou, elk, and bison migrate based on these cues. All animals navigate using some combination of electromagnetic signals, such as the angle of sunlight and the magnetic flux of the earth's electromagnetic field. All of the choices you make in life are, on multiple levels, driven by biological needs that you "sense" through your mind. When we introduce artificial forces, fields, and materials into our lives, they alter what we sense, and therefore what we think and what decisions we make. This is why if you wake someone up in the middle of the night, they will probably be grumpy. Meet that person out partying at 2:00 a.m. and they are likely to be friendly. What is the difference? To stay up until 2 in the morning, you are likely to be surrounded and inundated by strong light, music, food, and drink. Different environments provide our bodies with different signals, and this leads to different decisions.

What people fail to appreciate and control is the factors in their environment that influence their decision-making. We are taught to consider ourselves the masters of our own destinies, but decades of research in psychology and marketing have shown us how even the most intelligent, educated people are sometimes the most gullible. Modern corporations are waging psychological warfare on the public in an effort to extract as much wealth from them as possible. Some will object to my characterization of marketing as psychological warfare, but it is in many cases quite literally killing the customer. The average consumer today is trapped in cycles of addiction to anything from their cell phone to their smart watch to the contents of their refrigerator. The potential harms of modern conveniences have been largely down-played or outright ignored by public health authorities, who are more concerned with distributing and promoting preventive medicine that enriches pharmaceutical companies, doctors, and hospitals. Why are they not focused on helping Americans to eat a healthy diet and live a healthy lifestyle?

If the modern consumer is trapped, then we should ask, what forces keep them trapped? And how can they escape? My patients come to me out of a sense that they are trapped in their illness, and need my guidance to find a way out. They realize that their habits and choices are driving their disease, otherwise they would just continue taking pills and resign themselves to being sick forever. They do not know how to modify their environment to empower themselves with control over their health, and this is what I teach them.

Technology does not just trap humans, but animals as well.

Trapped by Our Desires

Ecological traps trick living organisms into making often fatal decisions. We humans inadvertently produce traps for other animals and plants, which we call ecological traps. Biologists first noticed this when studying the mating habits of certain insects. Insects cannot see water in the detail that we can, but they can see the difference between unpolarized and polarized light. Many insects lay their eggs in a calm body of water. Calm bodies of water polarize light, meaning that they turn the light waves to orient in the same direction, and this is how these insects select where to lay their eggs. This is a basic principle of physics that these organisms have turned to their advantage. They do not have the complex ocular structures that we do, and so when they see polarized light, they think, "that must be a calm body of water."

However, we make many things that polarize light. Polished headstones of marble or granite, asphalt driveways, windows, and much, much more all reflect and polarize light. Insects may mistake these things for calm bodies of water, and lay their eggs near or upon them. These insects are not able to distinguish between grandma's headstone and the pool of water she rests beside. They do not have the sensory organs, let alone higher reasoning abilities, to realize that laying their eggs on your windshield or grandma's headstone is a mistake. The eggs they lay on asphalt, windshields, headstones, and so on are doomed to death.

We are no different.

Consider a fourteen-year-old teenage boy on his cell phone in his room, at home. He is in a temperature-controlled house. Unbeknownst to him, this is why he has allergies. The constantly recirculating air is loaded with dust mites and pet dander, but he and his parents do not perceive this, and so they assume it is not a problem. He lives in a dark room most of the time, because he likes to play video games or play on his phone. His parents think he is just obsessed with the video game of the month, but it is more than that. He stays up until all hours playing video games or watching videos of beautiful women doing indecent things. He fails to develop social skills in this critical time. He cannot read body language cues, because he never interacts with other people. He never gets any sunlight and he only stops playing to eat packaged, processed food. He gains weight. Or, another common scenario, he never exercises and eats carbs instead of protein, and becomes scrawny and weak. He develops horrific acne due to his unhealthy lifestyle. He breathes through his mouth, which leads to lower intelligence, orthodontic problems, and crippling anxiety.

His parents learn to fear his dark moods and have no strategy to help him improve. His sleep finally becomes so disrupted by the artificial light at night and the lack of sun during the day, that he begins to struggle with fatigue. He becomes embittered against the world. Perhaps he wanders into an internet chatroom and is radicalized into a Nazi. Or a Communist. Or he learns to hate women, because they shun him for his acne and lack of social graces. Perhaps he descends into despair and takes his own life. Perhaps he shows up at his school with a gun and takes out his frustrations on his classmates. Perhaps he just persists in his quiet life of misery.

This is a story I have seen too often.

His sister is hardly better off. She too has allergies, and she too becomes a mouth breather. At fourteen, she is not interested in video games, but social media. The artificial light at night ruins her circadian rhythms, her sleep, and her mood. She develops anxiety. Her anxiety centers around her body image. She has severe acne, like her brother, and tries birth control. She gains weight. She stops birth control to try to lose the weight again. Her acne gets worse. She tries an antibiotic, but develops irritable bowel syndrome after taking it for six weeks. She becomes more and more self-conscious about her body image. She eventually reads that gluten may be the problem, so she goes on an elimination diet. This clears her skin and helps her to lose weight. She is less depressed about her body image, but she now has an unhealthy relationship with food. She starts to follow lots of social media influencers who are everything she feels she is not—thin with clear skin. Her role models are girls who, a generation ago, would have been shunned by society for impropriety. She gets an IUD and spends the next twenty years dating around, while looking forward to eventually settling down and having a family. She looks good and feels good, so long as she avoids gluten, but her irritable bowel syndrome remains a persistent issue. She finally does settle down, but has difficulty conceiving. She spends a hundred thousand dollars on fertility treatments. Perhaps she is successful. Perhaps not. She wonders what might have happened if she had not waited so long. Her children develop the usual illnesses that children today suffer from, like allergies, eczema, and recurrent ear infections. She wonders if her children's ailments are due to her decision to delay having children.

These two young people are typical of cases that I see every day in my practice. People today become trapped at a young age by corporations who will sell them anything, no matter the cost to their health. Children are inundated by advertising for unhealthy food. Young adults are inundated by advertisements for apps or video games. They are raised on fake food, under fake light, staring into devices that emit fake light, with little in-person interaction, which has been replaced by virtual relationships, and we wonder why they have never been sicker in body and in mind. They are then prescribed fake medicine for diseases they would not have, if only their doctors knew how to fix their diets, lifestyles, and environments. As Hippocrates said, "the greatest medicine of all is teaching people how not to need it." It is no mystery as to why modern people are so sick. Their doctors know nothing about being healthy.

Addicted to Bad Decisions

We are complex systems. Complex systems defy reductionist approaches to explain their inner workings. Why can one person eat the entire box of cookies and not gain a single pound, while other people can walk by a slice of cheesecake and gain weight? Why can one person stay up all night and function well the following day, while another is a stupefied zombie? Why can one person drink a six pack of beer without becoming intoxicated, while another may barely tolerate a single drink? Why are we all different? And how can we be so different, when we all share the same genome?

The answer is far more complicated than "genetics." If it were so simple, then twins would always share the same fate. They do not. In twin study after twin study, health outcomes between twins differ widely and depend predominantly on their environments. The modern world's healthcare crisis is truly due to hidden causes of disease in our modern environment. We become trapped by our own devices into choices that undermine our health. Modern diseases are the result of these ecological traps.

In the examples above, each of the siblings was entrapped by their primitive desires. These center around the needs for food, shelter, community, and the drive to reproduce. Junk food entraps us with flavor enhancers and artificial colorings. Video games entrap us with brilliant graphics and enticing "game mechanics" that are designed to be as addictive as possible. Pornography offers the illusion of intimacy and sexual gratification. Social media can provide us with social approval, but it can also create intense feelings of inferiority, jealousy, and anger. Alcohol offers us relaxation. Cocaine, amphetamines, nicotine, and other drugs all offer some kind of performance advantage or psychosocial benefit, regardless of their adverse effects. Birth control gives us the illusion of successful reproduction, without the responsibilities (babies) that usually come with it. Antibiotics can be life-saving, but they can also destroy your microbiome and are linked to many chronic health conditions.[96] The same can be said of any prescription drug. We live in a world where we can indulge in virtually anything to excess. Is it any wonder that our self-indulgent society is plagued by disease?

We are fascinated by how our bodies develop disease, and likewise how our bodies regain their health. Yet we know enough about life at this point to make some simple and pragmatic conclusions over what is healthy, and what is not. A moment or two playing video games is nothing, but a twelve-hour marathon is excessive. A chocolate chip cookie is a "treat," but the whole box is poison. We struggle with moderation, but largely because we create an environment in which moderation is difficult.

---

96   Queen, J., Zhang, J., & Sears, C. L. (2020). Oral antibiotic use and chronic disease: long-term health impact beyond antimicrobial resistance and Clostridioides difficile. Gut microbes, 11(4), 1092–1103.

This choice is easy to change.

This is the challenge of technology. How do we use it wisely? Just as modern food, medicine, air-conditioning, climate control, and transportation (to name a few) can entrap us in unhealthy habits, it can enable us to achieve new heights of performance and experience. This is why so many elite athletes, musicians, and soldiers use performance-enhancing drugs. A student popping an adderall before a test is taking a risk to improve their chances of success on the test—the risk is that of addiction, weight loss, and other health problems. The soldier using chewing tobacco on the field of battle may have faster reflexes and better coordination, and it may save his life. It may also addict him and, if he uses the wrong kind form of tobacco, give him tongue or throat cancer.

We constantly take risks that advance us toward reward, yet each risk carries with it the possibility of becoming entrapped in negative cycles of behavior. Entrepreneurs and students take on loans. Home-owners take on mortgages. Gamblers bet money on dice, sports, and cards. Everything that you do of consequence—eating, drinking, fighting, gambling, making love—entails both risk and reward. What risks we take depend upon what we know, or sense, and how it is integrated in our minds. When we do not perceive or understand the harms of risks relative to rewards, we can become trapped in these negative cycles of behavior. You can smoke packs of cigarettes a day and dodge cancer for decades (or die of something else), but this does not make smoking harmless. In many cases, "harms" are difficult to quantify, and are arguably negligible with certain doses or routes of administration.

Native Americans enjoyed such addictive substances as cocaine and nicotine before the arrival of European settlers, but they did not enjoy them in such excess as to create severe disease. The traditional way of using coca leaves is to chew them—not to dry them out, turn them into powder, and then snort them up your nose. The traditional way of using tobacco is in a pipe—not in a tightly rolled piece of paper loaded with all kinds of other additives, fillers, and flavorings.

"The dose makes the poison."

- Paracelsus

Any practice that can confer health and longevity can also be carried out to an extreme that creates disease and even premature death. The devil is in the details. This is why freedom is essential to good health. So-called public health "experts" do not understand what is good for all people at all times and in all places. They are not in a position to make better choices than you are. They are also easily corrupted by private interests (corporations and wealthy individuals or groups) that want to take advantage of their power to advance their own ends. In the end, their recommendations are designed to serve an 'average' person, thereby denying our unique and varying needs. By making blanket public health recommendations, government bodies alienate everyone, because no individual is average. Corporations have a strong incentive to promote blanket public health advice, such as mass vaccination, mass cancer screening, or mass water treatment, because whoever wins the contracts to the public health measures will gain a significant and durable stream of income.

Nicotine and cocaine are two colorful examples of the kinds of addictive substances that can enhance our performance, or cripple it. I am not advocating for their use, merely pointing out that high-achieving people often do use them to their material advantage. There is nothing subtle about the effects of these drugs, which is why they are so well known. What people do not appreciate are the myriad effects of the more mundane, sometimes subtle energies and choices that we make. How many minutes we spend staring into a screen each day. Where our air comes from. What kind of water we drink. There are many factors in our diets, lifestyles, and environments that may have profound health consequences that we are completely unaware of. Many people today say they have allergies to ancient staple foods, such as wheat. Yet many of these people do not test positive for allergies to these things, so are they truly reacting negatively to it? There are many food additives and pesticide residues in modern, processed foods, and many people unwittingly are reacting to these, rather than to the foods themselves. Many people create (fad) diets that are deficient in a wide range of nutrients, and then wonder why they develop symptoms of nutritional deficiencies. People think that their health devices, nutritional supplements, and hygiene practices are making them better, and yet when they give them up (which is something I frequently recommend), they often recover their health. In other words, what they thought was healthy was, in reality, unhealthy for them.

Why are we creating an environment in which it is so challenging to do the right thing? Where previously ordinary health and vitality seem like an elusive or even impossible achievement? We do this out of ignorance— ignorance of why we make decisions and of how our bodies fundamentally work. Once you are aware of this information, you can change your life for the better, overnight. Corporations have every reason to obfuscate this information, to keep you trapped in decisions that are bad for you and profitable for them.

People have been falling into these traps since the dawn of time. This is part of human nature. Ecological traps have always led to public health catastrophes, from ancient Rome to modern America, because they are far from obvious and they always involve things that people like.

"We learn from history that we do not learn from history."

- Georg Hegel

Humans have fallen into ecological traps since the dawn of time. Understanding how and why is the first step to avoiding them in the present and the future.

5. Victims of Our Own Success

Why Technology Can Make or Break Your Health

"Here we stand in this new world with our primitive brain, attuned to the simple cave life, with terrific forces at our disposal, which we are clever enough to release, but whose consequences we cannot comprehend."

- Albert Szent-Gyorgi

We are the most innovative animal on planet earth. We do not have sharp, hardened claws, or long, razor-sharp teeth. We do not have tough hides or scales. We are one of the softest, least formidable animals on earth. It is our ability to innovate that sets us apart. Our ability to speak, to think in complex ways, to reimagine our world, and then to make it so has given us mastery over our planet.

If we were less intelligent or lacked opposable thumbs, we would be restricted to a tropical and subtropical range, where we would be opportunistic hunters and foragers. Instead, we can range to the furthest poles of our planet, to the deepest corners of the oceans, and to peaks so high that no other animal dares to approach them. We have a miraculously long lifespan for an animal that lives on land. The longest living vertebrate (the Greenland shark) and the longest living mammal (the Bowhead whale) both live in the frigid waters of the North Atlantic. I do not think that is a coincidence.

Innovation has become one of our highest ideals. We revere scientists and inventors. Da Vinci, Einstein, and Newton are household names. We may also vilify them for enabling us to destroy each other on an ever expanding scale. Robert J. Oppenheimer, the father of the atomic bomb, quoted the Bhagavad Gita upon witnessing the first detonation of his creation, saying, "Now I am become Death, the destroyer of worlds."

Everyone appreciates the dangers of atomic bombs, guns, knives, and other weaponry. What is not so obvious are the insidious effects of many innovations upon our health. Just a few generations ago, doctors endorsed cigarettes, cocaine, dichlorodiphenyltrichloroethane (better known as DDT), and thalidomide. A few decades later, it is common knowledge that these products are dangerous.

We fell (as a species) for cigarettes, cocaine, DDT, and thalidomide, because they helped us to achieve short-term goals. The long-term ramifications are still with us. Our tendency to underestimate the consequences of our actions when short-term gain is possible has been a problem since the dawn of time.

One of the first examples of this was lead poisoning in ancient Rome.

How Lead Poisoning Hastened the Fall of the Roman Empire

The ancient Romans were one of the first civilizations to significantly alter their environment with their industrial activity. Data from ice cores in the Arctic show increased levels of heavy metals at the height of Roman power, when they would have been smelting large quantities of heavy metals like lead and iron.[97,98] Lead was favored by Romans due to its abundance and the ease with which it can be smelted. The Romans made pipes and lined aqueducts with lead. They lined their cookware with it. Lead was added to wine to sweeten it and used it as an ingredient in makeup. Lead was everywhere in ancient Rome.

When metal ores are mined, they have to be refined into pure metals. This process is known as smelting, and it entails a certain amount of environmental contamination. This contamination reached the Arctic via the atmosphere, where we find it in ice cores. A certain amount would have contaminated Roman air, water, and food. What impact this had on Roman health is a matter of debate amongst historians.

Exposure would have varied widely. How much wine a Roman drank, how often they applied makeup, what kind of makeup they applied, where they got their water, and where they lived would all have played a role in how much lead they would have been exposed to. A wealthy woman who applied lead makeup daily, preferred sweetened lead wines, and enjoyed fruit compotes cooked in lead-lined vessels might have had severe lead poisoning. Someone who preferred dry wines, did not apply makeup, and ate plain food would have had less exposure. Ironically, wealthier Romans would have likely had greater

97   Joseph R. McConnell, et al. (2018), Lead pollution recorded in Greenland ice indicates European emissions tracked plagues, wars, and imperial expansion during antiquity, Proceedings of the National Academy of Sciences, 115(22), 5726-5731.
98   Preunkert, S., McConnell, J. R., Hoffmann, H., Legrand, M., Wilson, A. I., Eckhardt, S., ... & Friedrich, R. (2019). Lead and antimony in basal ice from Col du Dome (French Alps) dated with radiocarbon: A record of pollution during antiquity. Geophysical Research Letters, 46(9), 4953-4961.

exposure than poor Romans.

How great was the exposure of the average Roman? Lead tends to deposit in bone, so bone levels of lead are accurate markers for overall lead exposure. We know that bones recovered from ancient Roman sites have lead levels three to four fold higher than those of bones recovered from sites predating the Roman Empire.[99] It is likely that many Romans did suffer from either acute or chronic complications of lead exposure.

Lead (and all heavy metals) damage the body by producing excessive oxidative stress and by interfering with the functions of metals like copper, zinc, molybdenum, and manganese. The body has no functions that rely upon lead. This means that any exposure to lead is poisonous, but small exposures will not cause significant symptoms. Chronic accumulation can lead to slow and insidious disease. Roman physicians did suspect that lead was toxic, even in small quantities. They documented cases of lead poisoning, though they could never quantify this disease as we can now.

One of the most dire effects of lead poisoning is neurodegeneration, or degeneration of the brain and nervous system. This may manifest insidiously as dementia in adults or as developmental delay in children. Heavy metal poisoning can mimic virtually any psychiatric disease, and victims often manifest bizarre behavior as their disease worsens.

As the Roman Empire declined, Roman historians documented bizarre behavior among emperors Nero and Caligula, among others. These accounts are difficult to confirm. In many cases, the only historical accounts we have of these emperors were left by people who bitterly despised them. This may have led them to unjustly characterize the emperors as insane. The question of whether or not lead may have driven ancient Romans mad is one we cannot settle with the data available, but it is certainly plausible.

Lead poisoning has since been described in exhaustive detail. We know exactly what it does to the body. Despite this, lead continued to be used widely in products until the last few decades. Even today, older homes have lead paint still on their walls, and for this reason infants and children are screened for lead poisoning. Lead was added to gasoline for years just to reduce engine knocking. Lead is still used in munitions, leading to the occasional case of lead poisoning in avid indoor shooters (or just shooters who are careless with lead munitions). Even after hundreds of years of learning about how toxic lead is, it took substantial efforts on the part of doctors, scientists, and environmentalists to reduce the public's exposure to lead. Just a few years ago, lead poisoning

---

99   Wexler, Philip. Toxicology in Antiquity. Academic Press, 2018. Page 490.

captured headlines once more, when the city of Flint, Michigan experienced the largest mass-poisoning in recent years.[100]

Lead is so obviously toxic that even ancient Roman physicians eventually recognized that it was a toxin, even without modern scientific methods. They first noticed its effects in those who worked with lead. As lead found its way into more products, and therefore into more Romans in greater and greater quantities, they began to notice its effects among those who lacked occupational exposures. Lead poisoning would have afflicted the most affluent Romans, who could afford to drink excessive quantities of sweetened wine or fruit compotes, to which lead was routinely added. Affluent Romans were also more likely to use make up that contained heavy metals, such as lead and arsenic.

The varying concentrations of lead in different products and different patterns of use would have resulted in sporadic lead poisoning cases in ancient Rome. There may also have been a contribution from lead plumbing. Two people leading practically identical lives might have had radically different exposures. A Roman who drank large quantities of sweet wine, ate lead-fortified fruit compotes, wore lead make-up, and drank water from lead piping might have extremely high exposure. Another, who drank the same amount of wine, wore the same amount of make-up, ate the same amount of fruit, and drank the same amount of water, might have virtually zero lead exposure. These details may make the difference between lead poisoning and good health. We will never know the extent to which lead poisoning contributed to the fall of the Roman Empire. How could we? The irony of ecological traps is that they usually trap those who can best afford them. Poor Romans would have struggled to afford wine, fruit compotes, and make-up. Only wealthy Romans could afford to poison themselves insidiously with lead. This is the problem with ecological traps – you are unlikely to realize that you are trapped until it is too late. This pattern has repeated itself throughout history.

How Technology Can Create Pollution, Malnutrition, and Disease

Many toxic substances and habits are more insidious than lead. Once the Roman Empire fell, lead levels declined significantly thanks to the reduction in smelting that took place. They rose again once medieval Europeans began to build new cities, nations, and civilizations. The same technologies that sickened

100   Ruckart, P. Z., Ettinger, A. S., Hanna-Attisha, M., Jones, N., Davis, S. I., & Breysse, P. N. (2019). The Flint Water Crisis: A Coordinated Public Health Emergency Response and Recovery Initiative. Journal of public health management and practice : JPHMP, 25 Suppl 1, Lead Poisoning Prevention(Suppl 1 LEAD POISONING PREVENTION), S84–S90.

the Romans sickened medieval Europeans.

With the industrial revolution, our capacity to poison ourselves reached new heights. The Romans could hardly have dreamed of the levels of air and water pollution that became normal in industrial Europe. Property rights, which have been a hallmark of Western law since Roman times, were used by industries to establish a "right" to pollute. The result is that for centuries the people of Europe suffered from premature disease and death that could have been prevented, if only they had protected their environment.

Malnutrition only worsened the health effects of Europe's excessive pollution. Canning and pasteurization were invented in the mid-1800's. These methods of food preservation have saved countless lives from hunger, but at the time, people did not appreciate that these methods also destroy many heat-sensitive vitamins. Albert Szent-Gyorgi, who won the Nobel Prize for discovering vitamin C, said of vitamins, "A vitamin is a substance that makes you ill if you don't eat it." Scurvy is the disease that results from vitamin C deficiency, with one of the manifestations being repeated and intractable infections. Urban populations in Europe were severely malnourished.

Food preservation has enabled us to eat extreme diets. We are the only animal on planet earth that can indulge in a non-local, non-seasonal diet. This is why we are the only animal on planet earth struggling with epidemics of diet-related diseases like diabetes and obesity. Malnutrition became a serious problem in the industrial revolution, and doctors quickly realized that eating an extremely limited diet of largely processed, preserved foods led to disease.

Malnutrition due to limited and processed diets was compounded by the toxic effects of air pollution. Air pollution consists of two chief components - gaseous pollutants and particulate matter. Gaseous pollutants include what are generally referred to as, "toxic chemicals." Your car's emissions are full of compounds like ozone, nitric oxide, and carbon monoxide that are toxic. The body can neutralize these, but it requires vitamins like vitamin C and E. These can easily be depleted by exposure to excessive pollution. Particulate matter, more commonly known as, "dust," can be inhaled and must then be processed by the body's immune system. This also requires resources and energy. Air pollution also blocks ultraviolet light from reaching the surface of the earth, and can therefore contribute to vitamin D deficiency. Water pollution also became a serious public health problem, with sewage and industrial wastes routinely contaminating public aquifers. The result was that urban populations in industrialized nations were malnourished by their diets, and poisoned by their air and water. This left them vulnerable to infection, and it is no coincidence that many of the world's worst epidemics have affected urban populations more severely than rural populations. It is also no coincidence that the disappearance of many infectious diseases followed major improvements in sanitation. Vaccination gets much of the credit for this, but clean air, water, and wholesome food deserve the vast majority of it.[101]

The negative health effects of pollution and malnutrition are obvious. Physicians of industrial Europe readily understood what was making their patients sick. Yet it took decades and centuries of reform, as well as major advances in fields of study like water sanitation and engineering, to clean up Europe and America's air and water. By the late 1900's, scientists had described the nutritional and toxic effects of every mineral, vitamin, amino acid, fat, oil, and carbohydrate you can find in the grocery store. Not surprisingly, life expectancy in industrialized nations soared. Never before in history had we been so far from the diseases that had affected our helpless ancestors. Ironically, industrializing nations like China are now just as polluted as America or Western Europe ever were. They are also struggling with malnutrition, obesity, and diabetes.

Soaring life expectancy, however, is now a thing of the past. Life expectancy in America is now declining.[102]

Why American Life Expectancy Is Now Declining

Why? If we know more about nutrition, sanitation, exercise, and medicine in general than ever before, then why would life expectancy be declining?

If you ask most doctors this question, they will point to the excessive dietary choices and sedentary lifestyle of most Americans. They will say that to be healthy, you just need to focus on, "diet and exercise." The finer details of this escape them, and they have little to offer in terms of exact recommendations to patients. Their recommendations often fail to get the desired results. Yet they are quick to blame patients, without examining why patients are making those choices. Americans are making these choices because their government makes it possible, not because they intrinsically want to. The government and the public health "experts" are the problem – not the American people.

What is it about modern diets and lifestyles that are crippling modern

---

101   Humphries, S., & Bystrianyk, R. (2013). Dissolving Illusions. Disease, Vaccines, and the Forgotten History, Kindle, 2587-2591.
102   Venkataramani AS, O'Brien R, Tsai AC. Declining Life Expectancy in the United States: The Need for Social Policy as Health Policy. JAMA. 2021;325(7):621–622.

people? Why do I spend hours counseling my patients about the specifics of their diets, lifestyles, and exercise routines that other doctors do not? We readily understand the matter of our bodies, we understand the interactions of light, sound, and electrical and magnetic fields with biological systems, and yet we struggle to integrate our technological advances with our biology in a way that optimizes health, rather than undermining it.

The reason that our health escapes us as a society lies in our reductionist approach to medicine and medical science. Our paradigm is broken, and that is why our modern medical institutions are failing to stop the rise of chronic diseases.

How should we think about health and disease? What should our criteria for what constitutes "healthy" practices, foods, or lifestyles be? Why is there so much controversy about these seemingly simple questions? How can we find clarity in a world of noisy sales people?

The short answer is that good health is an emergent property of complex systems. Once you understand what this means, the answers to many of your health and wellness questions will become clear.

6. Healthy by Nature

How Your Choices Determine Your Health

"The natural healing force within each one of us is the greatest force in getting well."

- Hippocrates

Your body is a complex system that absorbs energy, matter, and information from the environment in order to perpetuate your life, and to create new life. Your body can utilize all forms of energy and matter to varying degrees. You can combust matter to create energy, you can absorb energy to alter matter, and your body regulates its many systems and physiologic processes based on information (in the form of energy and matter) from the environment.

The key to understanding your own health is to understand complex systems. What are complex systems? Why do I begin a conversation about health by talking about complex systems? Complex systems consist of multiple interconnected systems, each of which have multiple variables that determine their function. Different properties of and processes within complex systems will emerge from the variables that determine the functioning of each system. For example, if you were to walk outside into bright, summer sunlight, and spend 20 minutes with your skin directly exposed, you would develop a tan. The process of tanning begins with ultraviolet light hitting the skin, where it creates a myriad of cascading effects. It can transform photo-sensitive vitamins, like vitamin A, into new compounds.[103] Each of these chemicals has unique effects on multiple body systems. It triggers the production of endocannabinoids and endorphins within the skin.[104,105] It can produce vitamin D. When you "feel"

103   Andersson, E., Rosdahl, I., Törmä, H., & Vahlquist, A. (1999). Ultraviolet irradiation depletes cellular retinol and alters the metabolism of retinoic acid in cultured human keratinocytes and melanocytes. Melanoma research, 9(4), 339–346.
104   Ouchene, L., Muntyanu, A., & Netchiporouk, E. (2020). Ultraviolet Radiation Seeking Behavior, Mediated by Endogenous ⍺-Endorphin, Has Addictive Features. Journal of Cutaneous Medicine and Surgery, 24(4), 414–415.
105   Slominski, A. T., Zmijewski, M. A., Plonka, P. M., Szaflarski, J. P., & Paus, R. (2018). How UV Light

the sun, what you are really feeling is the effects of different wavelengths of light on your skin and your eye. When light strikes your eye, the photonic energy is transduced into an electrical signal that is then transmitted to your brain. This signal drives your circadian rhythms, which in turn affect hormone and neurotransmitter synthesis, energy production, and tissue repair and regeneration. In response to ultraviolet light, the brain produces a compound called alpha-melanocyte stimulating hormone (alpha-MSH). This hormone triggers melanocytes in your skin to create more pigmentation; in other words, it generates a tan. But this is not the only effect of alpha-MSH. It confers a multitude of health benefits that have led people to embrace it as a remedy for many problems. When people hear the words "health" and "sunlight," many of them think; "skin cancer." But as we will discuss later, sunlight is necessary for good health due to molecules like alpha-MSH.

When you view the body as a complex system, statements like, "take magnesium for sleep", or "the sun causes skin cancer", suddenly appear overly simplistic at best and dangerous at worst. Any process or property within your body, such as a disease process, emerges from each of the variables that affect it. Take sleep as an example. When we go to sleep, the entire body enters a state of relaxation, cycling between different levels of sleep, during which the body repairs itself. This process requires properly synchronized circadian rhythms. These endogenous rhythms are orchestrated by environmental signals including light, electrical and magnetic fields, meal-timing, exercise, neurotransmitter and hormone synthesis and release, sound, air quality, breathing mechanics, hydration, and water quality.

How can each of these variables affect sleep? Is it really possible that how you breathe or what water you drink can radically alter the quality of your sleep, and therefore your health?

First, we have to consider that sleep quality is a spectrum. Everyone has had the experience of a bad night of sleep. Chronically poor sleep results in premature aging and disease. This is analogous to health. A lifetime of unhealthy habits leads to poor health, premature aging, and an early demise. A lifetime of healthy habits and wise choices inevitably lead to better health and prolonged life. It is the aggregate of these circumstances that determine our health or disease.

How Your Choices Determine Your Health

Touches the Brain and Endocrine System Through Skin, and Why. Endocrinology, 159(5), 1992–2007.

76

"Illnesses do not come upon us out of the blue. They are the consequence of daily sins against nature. When enough sins have accumulated, disease manifests."

- Hippocrates

We are not made or broken by single acts, but by the aggregate of those acts. The quality of our sleep, as the quality of any emergent process or property of our bodies (digestion, mentation, movement, hearing, sight, touch, taste, and smell, to name a few) is determined by what we do, not only at night, but during the day. And not just today, but everyday of our lives. Our bodies want to be healthy, we just need to give them nourishment and a healthful environment, and they will repair themselves.

When I consider different how our choices affect our health, I like to divide the physical world into the two sides of Albert Einstein's famous equation - $E = mc2$. Why? Because any physical variable that life contends with falls neatly on one side or the other, and can affect both sides. What are the energetic categories? They are light, sound, and the electromagnetic force. What are the material categories? They are air, water, food, and our personal care products that go on our skin or into our bodies.

How do these things affect sleep?

Air pollution can negatively affect sleep quality, particularly if the patient has severe allergies to the pollutants, such as pollen or pet dander. How you breathe is just as important as what you breathe. How you breathe is referred to as your breathing mechanics. People who chronically hyperventilate are always anxious. The worse their anxiety, the greater the toll it places on their sleep. Mouth-breathing is a hallmark of sleep-disordered breathing syndromes, which are strongly correlated with premature aging and disease. I have been amazed by how improving breathing mechanics during the day can translate into improved sleep at night. Air quality is just as important as breathing mechanics. People with chronic allergies, rhinitis, and sinusitis often have air quality problems, and wind up on a wide range of medications that can cause fatigue during the day or that can disrupt sleep at night. When we cultivate healthy breathing mechanics and good air quality, we can create healthy, restorative sleep.

Hydration is also necessary for healthy sleep because water is an essential ingredient in cellular repair and regeneration. This is why excessive thirst and urination are hallmarks of illness. Going to sleep thirsty is difficult, because water is vital to healthy sleep. Thirst often wakes people from sleep, as does the need to urinate. This means that if we are not hydrating at the right time and in the right quantity, we can ruin our sleep. Often, when normal hydration can be restored, we can restore normal sleep.

Food supplies the raw materials that mediate sleep. The hormones and neurotransmitters that are necessary to enter and create healthy, restorative sleep are ultimately derived from food. How your body turns those substrates into the necessary ingredients for sleep is based on signals received from your environment, such as light. You must optimize both nutrition and the environment to optimize sleep. I find nutritional imbalances in my patients on a regular basis, from mercury poisoning to vitamin A deficiency. We cannot predict what we will find. Low levels of glycine, GABA, magnesium, tryptophan, serine, B-6, B-12, folate, niacin, copper, or zinc might be found in someone with sleep problems. These nutrients are all vital to sleep, so a deficit in any of them can cause poor sleep. Likewise, elevated levels of glutamic acid, norepinephrine, epinephrine, dopamine, copper, or zinc can interfere with sleep. Any constellation of these findings might explain a sleep problem. It is not enough to correct levels of these nutrients, because sometimes the body is driving levels up or down to compensate for some kind of stressor. We must address the reason why the level is abnormal first. This takes time and a deep understanding of all the environmental factors that might create an imbalance in a given nutrient.

Personal care products are far less likely to disrupt sleep than these other factors, but people do develop some strange sensitivities to their personal care products that can affect their health. I have yet to see this affect sleep, but I have seen patients resolve years of fatigue simply by changing their personal care products. Who knows if this may have been due to subtle effects on their sleep?

What about the energetic side of the equation?

Light is the main time-keeper of the body. That is why you can stay awake for hours in front of a screen, but fall asleep in minutes after turning on an old-fashioned incandescent bulb and opening a book. Infrared and red light, when these frequencies hit the skin or eye, they generate melatonin.[106] Melatonin is known as the hormone of sleep, but it is truly the hormone of light. Light signals drive melatonin cycles throughout your body, and thereby determine your circadian rhythms. In addition to setting your body's clocks, melatonin turns on all of your rest and regeneration programs within your

---

106   Zimmerman, S. and Reiter, R. 2019. Melatonin and the Optics of the Human Body. Melatonin Research. 2(1), 138-160.

cells. Visible light during the day also drives melatonin synthesis, as well as the synthesis of other hormones and neurotransmitters.[107] Dim light during the day can cause lack of sleep at night. Light at night can disrupt normal melatonin rhythms, depriving us of sleep. Anyone can tell you that bright light at night keeps them awake, but few people appreciate the complexities of the optics of the human body that indirectly use light during the day to drive sleep at night. Where are we getting bright light at night? Screens that are feeding us a steady stream of anxiety-provoking news and media, that in turn poison our minds to disrupt our sleep. Light problems can create sleep problems, so often when we fix a patient's lighting environment, we can fix their sleep.

Sound can affect sleep. You may not realize it, but sound from things like planes, trains, and cars can all disrupt sleep architecture. You may never even realize it, because this can happen even without waking you up. Sound is a stress, just like light. Sound during the day and before bed can have an impact on sleep, long after it has been silenced. The tone of music you listen to over time will have a profound impact on your overall outlook on life and emotions. People who are depressed or anxious are often listening to depressing or anxiety-provoking music. Inaudible sounds, known as infrasound, can have profound impacts on our minds and bodies. People who live near wind turbines often report significant health issues arising after the construction of the turbines. This is due to "infrasound" - sound that cannot be heard, but nonetheless impacts the body. If we can correct the patient's sound environment, we can often improve their sleep. People often do not realize how sound is in fact ruining their sleep.

Electromagnetic fields are a frequent cause of poor sleep, due to their effects on circadian rhythms and melatonin. Anything that runs on electricity creates these fields, but the strength and nature of the field vary widely, which is why many people are unaware of these effects. The interaction of these fields with our bodies is complex. You may notice nothing when you pick up your cell phone. Someone else may notice that the hand they use their phone in or that they keep their smart-watch on develops an unusual type of eczema that goes away when they stop using it. They may notice that their headaches go away when they stop using smart headphones. I have had many patients report improvements in sleep when they put their phones on airplane mode and turned their wifi off before bed. These energies can interfere with the natural energetics of our minds, ultimately disrupting our sleep. These energies can

---

107   Hollwich, Fritz. The influence of ocular light perception on metabolism in man and in animal. Springer Science & Business Media, 1979.

affect our nervous systems,[108] they can affect the water in our cells[109,110], they can affect levels of hormones and neurotransmitters[111], and they can affect the signaling of neurons within our minds and bodies. There is no part of our physiology that is unaffected by them. What we need to know is how they are affected by them, and what to do about it. In addition, many patients report improved sleep when they spend time connected to the earth's electromagnetic field. This field is one of the main drivers of our circadian rhythms.[112] Without a healthy electromagnetic environment, we cannot have healthy sleep.

This is just the beginning of what we must address when it comes to creating healthy, restorative sleep. Plenty of people live in complete ignorance of these factors, and that is why the rates of sleep disorders and diseases that are linked to poor sleep are rising rapidly. Simplistic solutions to problems in complex systems like, "eat less and exercise more," or "take magnesium," or "don't eat meat," may provide a therapeutic benefit, but they inevitably fall short of solving the problem. They may also cause harm. We are tempted to engage in this kind of simplistic problem solving, because it is easy and often it is temporarily effective. However, it always compounds our problems over time. If you have a problem with your breathing mechanics, taking may successfully mask the symptoms for a while. However, it will only allow your breathing mechanics to continue to deteriorate, and eventually just taking magnesium will not mitigate the problems caused by improper breathing mechanics. If you have a magnesium deficiency, no amount of mind-body medicine, light therapy, breathwork, or hydration will resolve the problem. You must take magnesium. Over the long term, you must correct all potential causes of magnesium deficiency and eat a diet with adequate magnesium for your unique dietary needs.

When I began practicing, I had no real training in how to identify the causes of disease. Over the course of the past several years, I have come to appreciate how virtually any single factor in a patient's case can create or contribute to their illness. I have become more and more convinced that no one thing causes any given disease, but that disease is rather an emergent property or process of complex systems.

---

108   Havas, Magda. "Radiation from wireless technology affects the blood, the heart, and the autonomic nervous system." Reviews on environmental health 28, no. 2-3 (2013): 75-84.
109   Zhao, L., Ma, K., & Yang, Z. (2015). Changes of water hydrogen bond network with different external-ities. International journal of molecular sciences, 16(4), 8454–8489.
110   Fesenko, E., Gluvstein, A., (1995), Changes in the state of water, induced by radiofrequency electromagnetic fields, FEBS Letters, 367, 53-55.
111   Singh, S., Kapoor, N., (2014). Health Implications of Electromagnetic Fields, Mechanisms of Action, and Research Needs. Advances in Biology, 2014
112   Ghaly, M., & Teplitz, D. (2004). The biologic effects of grounding the human body during sleep as measured by cortisol levels and subjective reporting of sleep, pain, and stress. Journal of alternative and complementary medicine (New York, N.Y.), 10(5), 767–776.

"When one tugs at a single thing in nature, he finds it attached to the rest of the world.".

- John Muir

I have seen things like air, water, light, sound, or electromagnetic pollution affect my patients and cause disease. I have seen one fad diet after another fail to deliver results or even cause harm to patients. Only when we consider all the relevant factors to a patient's health can we maintain or restore good health to them.

Complex systems are self-correcting. When you correct the factors that are causing their dysfunction, they will recover naturally. This is why the sickest people today live in the wealthiest countries, while the healthiest people on earth often live on the edge of, or far from, these wealthy societies. When Weston A. Price traveled around the world in the early 1900's, he noticed that virtually any departure from traditional lifestyles and diets brought with it modern diseases.[113] Seemingly unimportant details of daily life carry profound consequences.

What is the traditional way of life? What does it have in common across cultures? There is little, if any, air pollution, and it is generally limited to smoke from camp fires. Clothing is all-natural. Food is obtained locally, to be eaten most when in season and in limited quantities if preserved by smoking or sun-drying. Exercise is a necessary part of life. It is often of low intensity and long duration. The heaviest thing you might pick up in nature is the carcass of a large animal. People lived in close connection to the earth, without electrictronic devices.

"Everything in excess is opposed to nature."

- Marcus Aurelius

Technology easily creates excesses in our lives. If we are not careful, these excesses can undermine our health and derail the complex systems that comprise our physical bodies. This is why chronic, preventable diseases are running rampant in our modern world. To understand what it is to be healthy,

---

113   Price, Weston Andrew. Nutrition and Physical Degeneration: A Comparison of Primative and Modern Diets and Their Effects. 1945.

we must start by defining what our natural state is. Failure to account for any element of our natural environment can derail a patient's efforts to recover their health. I have seen many patients and their practitioners ignore vital elements of their environment, such as air quality, water quality, or light, sound or electromagnetic pollution, not to mention their diet.

M = Air, Water, Food, and Personal Care Products

What we think of as "air" is simply a mix of gasses that bathe our planet. The earth's atmosphere is made up of nitrogen, oxygen, carbon dioxide, and trace amounts of other gasses. Plants turn carbon dioxide into oxygen and carbohydrates while animals turn carbohydrates and oxygen into carbon dioxide. Differences in temperature based on the abundance of water and the intensity of sunlight (not to mention geothermal energy) create what we call, "wind". The constant movement of the wind ensures that the air on our planet is of largely uniform quality, at least so long as we do not ruin it. High-energy ultraviolet light breaks down anything larger than a diatomic oxygen or nitrogen, or carbon dioxide, which is why the atmosphere consists mostly of these three gasses. At a much smaller scale, life creates gasses that have a smell. The fragrance of a flower, the scent of a woman, and the smell of a forest are all local phenomena. The closer you get to the source, the more intense the smell.

What we mean by "good air quality" is the natural state of air on planet earth. The only natural sources of air pollution are forest fires and volcanoes. The first air pollution of human origin came from the camp fires of our ancestors. They must have disliked the smoke as much as we do, but they loved the warmth and the opportunity to eat cooked food. Next, we must have created simple shelters. Many of these were temporary, simple shelters or tents. They may or may not have had adequate ventilation. Ventilation and air pollution have been two of the major driving factors for human disease since the dawn of time.

Air pollution is one of the main causes of disease today. We can produce so much pollution that we can even change the air quality of the atmosphere across the world. Prioritizing the air quality of your home is truly an investment in your health. You will notice that more expensive homes are naturally in less polluted areas - areas of elevation, away from sources of pollution (most sources of air pollution are also sources of noise pollution, and people hate both), and in areas where the prevailing winds bring them fresh air from over a pristine body of water.

Air pollutants fall into two categories - gaseous and particulate pollutants. Gaseous air pollutants include things like ozone, which is reported in air quality reports or indexes. These pollutants are little larger than the carbon dioxide we produce and the oxygen that we consume, which means that they can easily enter our bodies and cause damage to them. Particulate matter is much larger - we casually call it "dust." Both of them are produced by the combustion of petroleum products.

Chronic exposure to air pollution drives chronic diseases in an insidious way. The more energy the body expends trying to neutralize harmful air pollutants, the less it has to neutralize other causes of disease.

There is another, lesser known consequence of severe air pollution - lack of sunlight. Sunlight drives all the cycles of life on earth, including the production of hormones and neurotransmitters in humans and animals. Air pollution dims your world, which is another reason people are so keen to escape it. The modern epidemic of vitamin D deficiency is in part related to air pollution over our cities.

Population density drives pollution. The most polluted cities on earth are the most populated cities, and their most polluted neighborhoods are their most populated neighborhoods. "Good fences make good neighbors," but we cannot fence out bad air. We can only try to filter it.

If you can't escape air pollution by moving to a less polluted area, then filtration is your only option. Air filters come in all shapes and sizes, and utilize many different technologies to purify the air. Some of these introduce liabilities of their own, as is the case with UV-light filters.

Case Study:

A patient came to me with many vague complaints, including joint pain, shortness of breath, and abdominal pain. I asked what her home air filtration system was like. She told me that it included a large UV-light filter. UV light produces ozone and is used in air filters to destroy microbes and volatile organic compounds. However, ozone is also a signaling molecule for our immune system and a free radical. Anything the body uses to signal can be a poison, or a medicine. I told her to unplug her UV light filter - several weeks later, she noticed a substantial improvement in many of her complaints.

How much modern immunological disease is due to excess free radicals in our indoor air? I don't know, but you won't find UV light filters in my home.

We are not meant to inhale more than traces of many different natural substances. Just think about the scent of a flower. Under what circumstances would you smell the scent of the same flower every day, for weeks at a time? Yet this is exactly what people are doing with aromatherapy diffusers, air fresheners, and "scent sticks." The "musty" odor you smell in the forest on a fall day is generated by leaf mold on the forest floor. Bring that moisture inside thanks to a leaky pipe or loose faucet connection, and you may end up inhaling far, far higher concentrations of mold around the clock than you would ever be exposed to in nature.

Many people have no idea where their air is coming from, where it is going, or what it is picking up along the way, even within their own home. What it picks up along the way can ruin your health, as was the case with one of my patients in Virginia.

Case Study:

A young woman came to me hoping to lose weight and eliminate her crippling allergies. I asked her over and over again what the air quality was like in her home. She told me over and over again that there were no air quality problems. We ran a comprehensive allergy panel after weeks of trying to figure it out without testing. She tested positive for two molds. She then discovered that the air intake for her home was underneath the house, and that mold was growing all around it. She had been inhaling this mold for months. She had the mold removed and her symptoms went away. Many doctors would have just put her on inhalers or allergy shots for years, instead of getting to the root of the problem. All she had to do was inspect the underside of her house to figure out what was really ailing her.

Over the years, I have heard the strangest stories from people about their air quality. At the end of the day, everyone should know where the air they are breathing is coming from, how it is being transformed on its way to their bodies, and how it is being exchanged for fresh air. You cannot take for granted that your home is free of leaks, that your ducts are properly sealed and insulated, or that your heating and air conditioning units are clean and free of pollutants. You have to look.

You also have to be aware of how pets, plants, and pests can affect your air quality. Sometimes, this is something we would rather not look at.

Case Study:

A young mother contacted me for answers to her son's severe eczema. His eczema involved his arms and legs and was so severe that he was bleeding all over his clothes constantly. She had high-quality air filters. She used all organic and natural personal care products. He ate a pristine diet that was completely free of processed food. His mother had already tried eliminating many of the common allergens that cause eczema, like wheat and dairy. He had already been tested by an allergist, but all testing was negative. When they took a vacation to Florida, his eczema completely cleared. Why? It turns out he was allergic to the family dogs. The dogs now live in the garage - the boy's skin is virtually eczema free.

One of my standard recommendations to patients who have immunological problems, whether they are allergies, autoimmune diseases, or "mystery" illnesses, is to take a vacation. This case illustrates just how powerful this simple intervention can be. The simpler the vacation, the better. I strongly recommend camping trips with next to zero technology - nothing more than tents, camp fires, flashlights, and ice to keep your food cold. Such trips can reveal the impact of everything from pet dander allergies to technology addiction in striking ways.

I mentioned earlier that how you breathe is just as important as what you breathe. Physicians in ancient China recognized that the animals with the fastest breathing (respiratory) rate also have the fastest heart rates, and that they are the shortest lived creatures. The longest living mammal on earth is the Bowhead whale. They also noticed that the sickest patients tended to have the fastest respiratory rates. This led them to routinely recommend slowing the respiratory rate and decreasing the amount of air moved per minute.

We have always been fascinated by our breath, but few scientists, let alone physicians, have bothered to determine how we are supposed to breathe. The term "mouth-breather" is insulting because there is a well-documented connection between mouth breathing and lower intelligence quotients. Over two thousand years ago, Hippocrates said, "Mouth-breathing youths are sluggards." In nature, breathing through our mouths leads to suboptimal fitness. Why do people end up breathing through their mouths? The short answer is allergies and stress. Sinus congestion leads to mouth breathing, as it is the only other way to obtain air. Stressors in our environment can also trigger us to increase our breathing rate, which naturally stimulates mouth-breathing. In nature, a sudden stressful stimulus perceived through the eye or ears was a likely precursor to fighting or fleeing from a threat. By opening the mouth, we decrease resistance to air flow, and thereby increase the amount of air moved per minute without increasing the effort expended by the muscles of respiration. Observe the average person watching television, playing video games, or scrolling through social media. There is a good chance that the more engaged or stimulated (stressed) they are by their technology, the more likely they are to be mouth-breathing.

In our modern world, this has led to an epidemic of silent hyperventilation. This is a well-described clinical syndrome that, sadly, modern clinicians have not been trained to recognize or treat.[114] This diagnosis has many skeptics and detractors in the ranks of so-called "scientific" medicine. Despite their skepticism, the benefits of nasal breathing and of slowing the respiratory rate are well-documented. A Russian physician named Vladimir Buteyko documented these benefits during the latter half of the 20th century.[115] His work has since been brought to the United States and the Western world in general, where hyperventilation is an epidemic.

When we breathe too much per minute, we blow off too much carbon dioxide. Carbon dioxide does two very important things for our physiology. It opens our blood vessels and causes oxygen to be kicked off hemoglobin, allowing it to be consumed for energy generation. When we hyperventilate chronically, we have lower levels of carbon dioxide in the blood, and therefore sub-optimal blood flow throughout the body.

What are the symptoms of hyperventilation syndrome?

Cold hands and feet

Shortness of breath

Fatigue

Brain fog

114   Brashear, Richard E. "Hyperventilation syndrome." Lung 161, no. 1 (1983): 257-273.
115   Bruton, Anne, and George T. Lewith. "The Buteyko breathing technique for asthma: a review." Complementary therapies in medicine 13, no. 1 (2005): 41-46.

Poor sleep

Lack of ability to focus

Anxiety

Depression

Does this sound familiar? How can one bad habit cause so many clinical manifestations? Your hands and feet get cold because they don't have adequate blood flow. You feel short of breath because carbon dioxide relaxes and opens your airways. You feel tired because oxygen cannot be utilized properly. You have brain fog, fatigue, depression, and an inability to focus because blood flow to the brain is compromised. This is also why sleep quality suffers with hyperventilation.

Chronic hyperventilation leads to a cascade of effects that is eventually seen in every organ.

Case Study:

A young mother came to me for help with postpartum depression. She had been hospitalized for depression and suicidality multiple times in the past. Her lab results indicated a number of nutritional deficiencies, but I also noticed she was breathing through her mouth. Within just three weeks of starting magnesium supplements and a breathing protocol, she lost several pounds and reported a significant improvement in her mood. Hyperventilation can actually drive losses of magnesium in the kidney. Did her mouth-breathing cause her magnesium deficiency? Did it cause her depression? Or was her depression due to magnesium deficiency? Either way, the treatment protocol is the same - treat the breathing mechanics and the low magnesium at the same time.

Untreated hyperventilation syndrome is responsible for great suffering in our modern world. What is most tragic about this is that treating it is completely free. This is why I spend a great deal of time educating patients about the importance of proper breathing mechanics.

Case Study:

A young mother with previous diagnoses of Lyme disease and multiple sclerosis came to see me after every other practitioner had failed to deliver results. She was disabled and being cared for by a family member. I recommended that she work on her breathing mechanics, while also taking a regimen of supplements based on her lab results. She did take the supplements, but she did not work on her breathing mechanics. Months later, she returned for follow-up. She had seen no improvement and in fact had continued to deteriorate. I further advised that she work on her breathing mechanics. She is now in hospice care. I will always wonder what might have happened if I had reached her sooner. I have concluded, based on her case and others, that those who will not fix their breathing mechanics will never fix their health.

Hyperventilation is part of the breathwork practices of many new health and wellness routines, like Wim Hof breathing. Hyperventilation for short periods does have a place, but carried to an extreme over a long time, it is disastrous to good health. I use it as a targeted intervention only in select cases. For the most part, the world is chronically hyperventilating, and it is a major public health problem. Sadly, authorities are more focused on things like vaccines, colonoscopies, mammograms, and pap smears, none of which are free, and all of which carry risks of potential harm.

Our lack of activity is partly to blame for our epidemic of hyperventilation. People living in the wild naturally exert themselves to the point of breathlessness all the time - this improves your tolerance for carbon dioxide and reduces your respiratory rate (essentially curing hyperventilation). People naturally love spending time in and around water. Holding your breath under water (free diving) is one of the best ways to improve your respiratory mechanics (and cure hyperventilation).

The air we are breathing and the way we are breathing are both being ruined by modern technology. We move more air into and out of our lungs than we drink water or eat food each day. Our air quality is vital to our good health and longevity.

Hydration and Water Quality

Water is vital to life, yet few people appreciate its true significance. Plants combine water and carbon dioxide to produce carbohydrates, making water vital to all photosynthetic life. What is most remarkable about water is not this simple chemistry, but quantum mechanical properties. In the 1960's, a scientist named Gilbert Ling, PhD pointed out that the energy produced by the mere combustion of food into carbon dioxide and water could not possibly meet the energetic needs of the cell. When food is combusted by a cell, the energy released is stored in molecules like adenosine triphosphate (ATP), which the cell then breaks down again to generate energy. Yet the energy produced by the cell through combustion does not produce enough ATP to meet the minimal metabolic needs of the cell. In other words, to say that a cell can function using only the chemical energy produced by the combustion of food is like saying that a car that only gets 30 miles to the gallon can go 1,500 miles on just 10 gallons of gas.

Most scientists ignored Ling's work, but a number of them carried on his work and confirmed his findings. Ling had hypothesized that the cell used water to store and generate energy, rather than just ATP. This relied upon principles of quantum mechanics that were nascent at the time of Ling's work. Only in the past few decades have we had the instrumentation and the experimental evidence to confirm what Ling hypothesized years ago. In recent years, the founding editor of the journal, "Water", Gerald Pollack, has written two books on this topic that outline the volumes of scientific support for Ling's theory.[116,117]

Most doctors and scientists to this day are unaware of this research, but the implications of these findings are far-reaching. The combustion of food into water and carbon dioxide produces more than mere matter - it produces light. This is no different than the combustion of wood (cellulose) into carbon dioxide and water in a fire, or of gasoline into carbon dioxide and water in an internal combustion engine. The frequencies of light produced are generally within the red and infrared range. This is what makes organisms with high metabolic rates "warm-blooded" - the infrared light produced by this combustion heats the body. What Ling, Pollack, and others have found is that these frequencies of light "structure" water, and that without this structuring effect, life falls apart.

Life does not just depend upon "water." It depends upon light and water working together to drive its vital functions. This makes an adequate and healthy water supply essential to life. Two things can ruin water. The first are contaminants, such as toxins or infectious agents, and the second is a lack of or proper mineral content.

116   Pollack, Gerald H. Cells, gels and the engines of life: a new, unifying approach to cell function. Seattle, WA: Ebner & Sons, 2001.
117   Pollack, Gerald H. "The fourth phase of water." Ebner & Sons Publishers, Seattle, Washington (2013).

Modern water supplies are woefully contaminated with everything from antibiotics to synthetic hormones. This is because municipal (city) water authorities make no money and have no incentive to do more than just make sure that water flow is continuous and that it is "safe." Safe does not mean healthy, it just means "not dangerous." Sadly, we are now even facing problems with basic water quality, such as we have seen in Flint, Michigan. The city faced an epidemic of lead-poisoning due to negligence on the part of certain government officials. This situation took years to remedy.[118]

If you still trust your local civil authorities to ensure that you have "safe" water to drink, you may end up struggling with lead-poisoning like the poor citizens of Flint. I think it is prudent to take matters into your own hands.

Besides which, some of the chemicals being added to our water are far from innocent. Municipal water authorities generally add fluoride to water for the purpose of improving dental health, and chlorine to the water for purposes of disinfecting it. The problem with this is that fluoride has harmful effects upon other systems of the body. Fluoride is well known to interfere with the metabolism of other vital minerals like magnesium and iodine,[119] both of which are essential for thyroid health. Today, we are dealing with an epidemic of low thyroid hormone levels. Is this due in part to the fluoride in our modern water supplies? I have seen patients successfully reduce their doses of thyroid hormone once they stopped drinking fluoridated water. Is this coincidence or causation? The data for its efficacy in supporting dental health is also questionable.[120] Many world experts on fluoride and public health have come to criticize the practice of adding fluoride to water.

I filter my municipal water through a reverse osmosis filter. This type of filtration eliminates all small chemicals and metals from your water, leaving you with clean, pure drinking water.

However, we need to consider what water contains in nature. In nature, all fresh groundwater contains a certain amount of mineral content. The most common minerals are calcium, potassium, and magnesium, followed by elements in much more trace amounts, such as lithium, strontium, copper, zinc, molybdenum, and manganese. Our bodies are best adapted to waters that are rich in these elements. This is why we consistently see health benefits to drinking mineral (or "hard") water in a variety of studies. For example, the

118   Hanna-Attisha, Mona, Bruce Lanphear, and Philip Landrigan. "Lead poisoning in the 21st century: The silent epidemic continues." American journal of public health 108, no. 11 (2018): 1430-1430.
119   Waugh D. T. (2019). Fluoride Exposure Induces Inhibition of Sodium/Iodide Symporter (NIS) Contributing to Impaired Iodine Absorption and Iodine Deficiency: Molecular Mechanisms of Inhibition and Implications for Public Health. International journal of environmental research and public health, 16(6), 1086.
120   Walters, C., 2006, Minerals For The Genetic Code

more lithium in your drinking water, the lower your risk of suicide.[121] The more magnesium in your drinking water, the lower your risk of heart disease.[122] These are important factors for health that everyone should be aware of.

The practice of drinking "pure" water - devoid of these life-giving minerals - generally leads to de-mineralization of the body. I routinely see low mineral levels in patients who have been drinking pure water, instead of mineral water. Many reverse osmosis units come with a re-mineralization unit that you replace once yearly. Without adequate minerals in water, people tend to develop mineral deficiencies.

Case Study:

A young man came to me complaining of depression, anxiety, lack of ability to focus, and a vague sense of "not feeling right." His labs were notable for low levels of zinc, copper, magnesium, and manganese. I recommended repletion with organ meats, shellfish, and nuts and seeds, and re-mineralization of his water with a solution that also contained some lithium. His depression soon thereafter lifted. He even reported feeling sort of "addicted" to his re-mineralization solution. His mineral levels are now nearing the normal range and he is happier than ever before.

In my clinical practice, I will recommend various re-mineralization protocols depending upon a patient's labs. This is yet another way in which I customize the patient experience to deliver results for my patients.

Many people are fond of drinking spring water, thinking that this is somehow superior to purified water. However, there are some cases in which spring water may actually contain chemicals or heavy metals that are injurious to your health. To make things worse, these spring waters are commonly packaged in plastic bottles that leech endocrine disrupting chemicals like phthalates and BPA into the water.

Case Study:

A young mother contacted me for help with severe postpartum fatigue and depression. We tested her levels of heavy metals and found that her blood

121   Kapusta, N. D., Mossaheb, N., Etzersdorfer, E., Hlavin, G., Thau, K., Willeit, M., Praschak-Rieder, N., Sonneck, G., & Leithner-Dziubas, K. (2011). Lithium in drinking water and suicide mortality. The British journal of psychiatry : the journal of mental science, 198(5), 346–350.
122   Jiang, L., He, P., Chen, J., Liu, Y., Liu, D., Qin, G., & Tan, N. (2016). Magnesium Levels in Drinking Water and Coronary Heart Disease Mortality Risk: A Meta-Analysis. Nutrients, 8(1), 5.

level of arsenic was slightly elevated. She lives in a region with high arsenic levels and was drinking spring water. She switched to reverse osmosis water and immediately her baby stopped spitting up. This is why I do not routinely recommend spring water.

Modern water supplies are full of contaminants and are unfit for drinking. What is perhaps worse than what we find in our municipal water is what people purposefully add to their water in the form of sweeteners, stimulants, and sedatives.

The Hazards of Modern Beverages

Not long ago, all we had to drink was water and mother's milk. Then we invented herbal teas. Somewhere along the line, we discovered Camilla sinensis, which falls into two categories - green and black tea. Today, you can walk into a grocery store and buy fermented tea (kombucha), iced tea, sweet tea, green tea, black tea, coffee, iced coffee, fruit juice, vegetable juice, wine, beer, soda, and sparkling water. You can sweeten it with aspartame, stevia, xylitol, cane sugar, fruit sugar, coconut sugar, white granulated sugar, or corn syrup, just to name a few. You can flavor it with syrups infused with herbs and spices, or you can add coconut milk, hemp milk, cashew milk, macadamia nut milk, almond milk, or walnut milk. You could also stick to the more traditional dairy, of which there are so many varieties. You could choose heavy cream, half and half, butter, skim, 2%, whole, and you could pick homogenized or unhomogenized, pastured or factory-farmed, organic or non-organic. If you are really feeling adventurous, you could even try goat milk.

Consider the complexity of the average beverage coming off the line of the coffee shop around the street from you. Municipal (tap) water, which is loaded with chemical contaminants, is used with little or no filtering to improve its quality. It is usually heated by an aluminum heating element, conferring a small amount of aluminum into it. It may be heated and stored in a plastic container, which will leach plastic into it. The raw ingredients, aside from water, may include any number of artificial ingredients, such as artificial flavorings, colorings, or preservatives, each of which can have untoward effects on your health. A large coffee drink can have as many calories as a nutritious meal, without any of the nutrients that you truly need to be healthy.

Is it any wonder that what modern people are drinking is making them sick?

Case Study:

A young woman with a long and complicated medical history came to me seeking a second opinion on why she was so sick. A toxicology panel I perform on every patient came back with an extreme elevation in levels of plastics in her blood. She told me she drank lots of bottled water. Many patients of mine drink bottled water, but not all of them have elevations in plastic chemicals in their blood. I asked what kind of bottles she was drinking from. She was drinking from the soft, grey one-gallon plastic bottles. When you open one of these bottles, you can easily smell the plastic. People assume this doesn't matter. How much it matters is a difficult question to answer - we may never know. I won't touch anything that comes out of those soft, grey plastic bottles. I minimize my consumption of beverages bottled in plastic and aluminum. I choose glass when I can.

What can go wrong with what we add to our beverages? We can inadvertently add toxins, like aluminum, to them. The most common sources of exposure are aluminum cans and aluminum heating elements in coffee makers and electric tea kettles. Many food additives have direct toxic effects. These are still controversial in modern medicine. Many doctors and experts dismiss the dangers of things like monosodium glutamate, sulfites, artificial food colorings, aspartame, and many more. However, there are also many patients who will clearly tell you that they feel worse when they ingest these foods, and better when they avoid them. It is difficult to prove or disprove causation in these circumstances.

Case Study: :

A young woman with acne, severe irritable bowel syndrome, and intractable vomiting came to me looking for help. I recommended that she eliminate processed food, despite having no evidence that she had food allergies or intolerances. A few weeks later, her intractable nausea was gone and her gastrointestinal symptoms had almost completely abated. I am amazed by the fact that more doctors don't recommend simple, effective interventions like elimination diets to their patients, when results like this are common. I cannot know if she improved by eliminating something she was eating or drinking. Regardless, she got better and that is what matters.

Case Study:

Another young woman came to me for fatigue. She was a self-described, "workaholic," who had spent the past few decades starting a very successful business. I recommend to all of my patients that they eliminate all caffeine and alcohol for the first two weeks of working with me. She was shocked to discover, upon stopping caffeine, that she had more energy. She started sleeping better and waking feeling more rested. People often don't realize that they are not sleeping well at night, because they are drinking caffeine too late in the day.

I make two fundamental recommendations to patients as to what they drink. First, that they should drink mineral water, with nothing else added to it. Second, they should eliminate alcohol and caffeine for at least two weeks.

The results of these two simple recommendations have been remarkable clinical improvements in patients who had "tried everything."

"Water is life's matter and matrix, mother and medium. There is no life without water."

- Albert Szent-Gyorgi

Water and light work together to make energy within our cells. Life starts with air (oxygen and carbon dioxide), which combust with water to produce light. This makes light the third vital input to our bodies, and one of the major determinants of health or disease. Light shapes life.

How is it shaping yours?

Diet and Nutrition

More has been written on the topic of food and health than perhaps any other. Hippocrates said, "Let food be thy medicine." This is a quote that is often repeated, because you can sell people food, herbs, and nutritional supplements. The profit margins to be had in selling people "food" are remarkable. This has led to the vast world of information and disinformation regarding food.

What should we eat? This is one of humanity's favorite and most hotly debated questions. We are the only animal on planet earth that eats a non-local, non-seasonal diet composed of highly processed, artificially preserved foods. Is it a coincidence that we struggle with countless diseases linked to malnutrition? I find this profoundly ironic.

How can we gain clarity on this issue? If your goal is to eat in such a way as to live for a long time, you should study the diets of people who live for a long time. These studies have not shown a single diet to be superior to any other. The vegetarians, vegans, carnivores, pescatarians, and fruitarians will (probably) continue to argue for the rest of time over what to eat, but in the end, the answer depends upon the patient.

An American dentist named Weston A. Price became interested in this question in the mid-1900's. He was struck by the number of children presenting to his clinic with crowded teeth and cavities. He undertook a journey around the world to examine how traditional diets protected people from modern dental problems. He studied almost a dozen different groups living in remote parts of the world, and eating the same foods their ancestors had eaten, prepared in the same way, for hundreds of years. He found that those eating their traditional diet had perfect teeth and strong, healthy facial bones. Those who had adopted modern foods, such as refined sugar, had fallen victim to malformed facial bones, crowded teeth, and cavities. His book, "Nutrition and Physical Degeneration," is a seminal work in the field of medical anthropology. Sadly, most doctors are unfamiliar with his work.

Price documented in great detail that people eating radically different diets could still enjoy good health. The Inuit and Eskimo could not eat a more different diet than Polynesian islanders or Peruvian mountain villagers. When we look at nutritional profiles of different foods, there are a wide variety of different sources. These vary seasonally. For example, most people think of citrus and other fruits as the best sources of vitamin C. This is true. If vitamin C deficiency is fatal, then how do people in places like Alaska or Greenland survive the winter, in which no fruits grow? The Narwhal is one of the first whales to migrate north through the sea ice in Alaska as it breaks up in the Spring. The Eskimo[123] have long hunted Narwhal at the first opportunity, coming south over the breaking sea ice to meet the northward migrating whales. The first thing they eat is the Narwhal skin, which is rich in vitamin C.[124] When people abandon their traditional ways of eating, they often abandon the chief sources

123   Lee, D. S. & Wenzel, G. W. (2004). Narwhal hunting by Pond Inlet Inuit: An analysis of foraging mode in the floe-edge environment. Études/Inuit/Studies, 28(2), 133–157.

124   Mullie, Patrick, Tom Deliens, and Peter Clarys. "Vitamin C in East-Greenland traditional nutrition: a reanalysis of the Høygaard nutritional data (1936-1937)." International Journal of Circumpolar Health 80, no. 1 (2021): 1951471.

of vital nutrients. It is easy for the average person today to go to the grocery store and walk out with nothing that contains appreciable quantities of vitamin C. I have diagnosed scurvy for this reason numerous times in my career. Sadly, patients and doctors are routinely unaware of the fundamentals of nutrition. This is convenient for the pharmaceutical industry, which profits greatly from the sale of drugs to treat diseases that are fundamentally dietary in nature.

What is clear is that people who live a long time in good health eat a variety of different foods. One of the trends in modern society has been toward a restricted dietary template. People tend to cut out entire food groups, or focus on a few instead of a variety of food groups. Many people go weeks or months without eating a single nut or seed. Others never eat legumes. Others never eat fish. This invariably leads to nutritional deficiencies and imbalances, and disease. It is also easy to over-consume certain foods. A few tablespoons of oil can move your diet from low-fat to high-fat. A handful of nuts can do the same thing. It is remarkable how much of a difference this can make clinically.

What is food? Food is made up of the elements of the periodic table. Within different food groups, we see radically different concentrations of nutrients. For example, you would have to eat several large heads of romaine lettuce to get as much folate as you get from one cup of black beans. You would have to eat bowls of oatmeal to get the same amount of fat as you could get from one egg yolk. Walnuts have nine times as much omega-3 fatty acids as sockeye salmon.

It is these seemingly inconsequential nutritional differences that lead to nutritional imbalances, deficiencies, and diseases. People, even the highly-educated and health-conscious, often have no idea what they are actually eating. For the most part, they eat things because they heard that they are "good," for them, with no concept of how much to eat in relation to everything else they might eat.

Case Study:

A 56-year-old woman came to me for weight loss. She was obese and knew she had to change something. She had tried ice-bathing, a ketogenic diet, and eating lots of seafood, but was not losing weight. Her labs revealed deficiencies in nutrients mostly coming from plants. I recommended she abandon her ketogenic diet that was rich in seafood and animal protein, for a temporary vegan diet. She promptly lost 17 pounds in 17 days. She has since then leveled out to losing one pound each week over 26 weeks, for 26 pounds of weight loss total.

Case Study:

A 45-year-old man presented with difficulty losing weight. He started to track his diet and realized he was getting hundreds of calories a day from wine. He was getting hardly any protein, plenty of fat, and plenty of carbohydrates. This is a recipe for weight gain. I recommended that he stop drinking wine altogether and adopt a ketogenic diet with almost twice the protein he had been getting each day. He lost ten pounds over a period of about a month.

These two cases illustrate that you can achieve better health with different diets, based on the patient's unique context. There is no "one size fits all" diet in my practice. There are variations on all the available themes. I will happily recommend veganism and a ketogenic, high animal-fat diet in the same day. These recommendations are always based on laboratory data and the patient's unique context. Why should two people in different environments, with different genetics, different life histories, different stress levels, and different medical problems eat the same diet?

What about adverse reactions to food or chemicals? Adverse reactions generally fall into the categories of allergic reactions, autoimmune reactions, intolerances, and sensitivities. This is another important point. Gluten is a prominent example. So many people today have labeled themselves as "gluten intolerant," but when we closely examine the ingredients in gluten-containing foods, they often contain far more than just gluten. The average loaf of bread contains not only flour from a grain (containing gluten), but also preservatives, natural and artificial flavors, dough conditioners, anti-humectants, anti-oxidants, sweeteners, vitamins, iron, and sometimes even artificial colorings. Each of these ingredients was made in a lab or refined in a factory. They might contain traces of industrial chemicals, pesticides, molds, fungi, bacteria, and more.

How do our bodies react with these many different ingredients? How our immune systems react with different chemicals continues to evade our simplistic methods of quantification. For example, until recently it was thought that the immune system did not produce antibodies against sugars or carbohydrates. The discovery of red meat allergy disproved this.[125] There are other natural phenomena that defy our understanding with our current instruments and science. For example, how does a shark smell blood through miles and miles of ocean? How does an animal migrate back to the spot it was born, to give birth or mate again, year after year? The short answer is "the electromagnetic force." Animals can sense changes in electromagnetic forces

---

125   Chandrasekhar, J. L., Cox, K. M., & Erickson, L. D. (2020). B Cell Responses in the Development of Mammalian Meat Allergy. Frontiers in immunology, 11, 1532.

with far greater sensitivity than humans can.[126] This is how they navigate. We navigate using this magnetic sense as well, but our geolocation methods do not approach the sensitivity and precision of other organisms. I believe that the immune system has ways of reacting to stimuli that defy our current methods of quantification.

One of the greatest frustrations of my patients with conventional medical care is the lack of interest in why they are reacting to a given food or chemical. Doctors, for the most part, stop at labeling someone as sensitive, intolerant, or allergic. They do not seek to understand why. In conventional terms, allergies are based on immunological reactions with immunoglobulin E, basophils, and eosinophils. This is a very narrow definition and likely covers less than 5% of all negative reactions to foods or environmental stimuli. Autoimmune reactions, such as Celiac disease, can be triggered by foods or chemicals as well. In Celiac disease, gluten triggers the body to react to the body's own tissues. This can cause symptoms affecting virtually any organ system. For example, there are proteins in the brain that are similar to another protein in gluten-containing grains, called gliadin. If the body begins to attack gliadin, it may also attack the cells of the brain. The result has been called, "gluten ataxia" or "gluten psychosis."[127] Patients present with a wide variety of neurological and psychiatric symptoms. This may explain why so many people with autoimmune diseases, such as multiple sclerosis, Crohn's disease, ulcerative colitis, and more have found value in eliminating gluten from their diets. This does not mean that gluten avoidance is for everyone.

Why should gluten be special? It is only one of countless proteins in our diets. Research into gluten sensitivities began in the 1950's, but has only recently begun to elucidate the full extent of Celiac disease and gluten sensitivity. If it has taken us this long to understand how one protein, from one common food affects our health, how many other diseases are the result of other proteins in other foods?

This is why doctors have recommended dietary modifications, including elimination of certain foods, since the dawn of time. The Hippocratic Oath specifically states that the physician will prescribe a specific diet to the patient, based upon their case. Elimination diets eliminate ingredients or foods either one at a time or in groups. These diets have become increasingly popular as the amount of processed food we eat has risen, for two key reasons. First, more and more people are having immunological reactions to their food - generally referred to as food allergies. Second, there are more and more ingredients

---

126   McFadden, J, Al-Khalili, J, 2014, Life On The Edge.
127   Hadjivassiliou, M., Sanders, D. S., Woodroofe, N., Williamson, C., & Grünewald, R. A. (2008). Gluten ataxia. Cerebellum (London, England), 7(3), 494–498.

in our food, specifically food additives, that have a wide range of biological effects, many of which can trigger symptoms that people then think of as food allergies. The result is that more and more people are finding value in eliminating specific foods or food groups.

The downside of elimination diets is that they can lead to nutritional deficiencies. I commonly see signs of nutritional deficiency in patients who are eating a restricted diet. We must either use a supplement or introduce a new food that they will tolerate to remedy the deficiency. The longer a restrictive dietary pattern continues, the more deficiencies tend to appear and the worse they become. This is why I see so many people who have been on complex elimination diets for months or even years, presenting with worsening disease despite strict adherence to their dietary regimen. Elimination diets are a double-edged sword. They do not guarantee health and patients often feel better, rather than worse, when we reintroduce foods they had previously eliminated.

Many food reactions are due to an inability to digest certain foods. Some people lack the digestive enzymes, stomach acid, or bile salts necessary to digest their food. This is another common cause of what are wrongly termed, "food allergies." These patients tend to avoid complex foods, particularly those that contain anti-nutrients. Anti-nutrients are things like phytates and lectins that plants produce to discourage animals from eating them. This is why eating raw or sprouted beans is a recipe for a day in the bathroom. However, high heat, pressure, changes in acid-base balance, or hydration can neutralize these anti-nutrients. They can also be neutralized by enzymes from our digestive tract and by adequate stomach acid. This is why most people eat beans, milk, and gluten with impunity, but some people strictly avoid them based on the symptoms they develop upon eating them. Lactose intolerance is the classic example that is easiest to understand. In lactose intolerance, the body does not produce the enzyme lactase, which breaks down lactose. When you take a lactase supplement or drink lactase-fortified milk, the problem disappears. These are not food allergies – these are food intolerances.

Food sensitivities occur when the body is sensitive to a given chemical within a food. Monosodium glutamate is a classic example. Monosodium glutamate is a food additive that most people have no idea is present in many of their favorite foods. However, some people react to it with a wide variety of symptoms, including headaches, flushing, palpitations, anxiety, and brain fog. Caffeine is another common example. Some people are not allergic to a specific food, but they are sensitive to a chemical. What determines our sensitivities is our unique biochemistry. Our nutritional status and environment will modulate what we react to, because these things affect how our bodies react to chemicals. This is why many people notice a difference in the severity of their food sensitivities over time and in different environments.

Many negative reactions to food are due to hidden infections in the gut. I have been astonished by the bacteria, yeast, and parasites that I have found in my patients. Frequently, eradicating these infections with the proper mix of anti-bacterials, anti-fungals, and anti-parasitics leads to complete resolution of symptoms. However, this must be undertaken with an appropriate protocol to rebuild the gut lining and the microbiome, otherwise the pathogens are likely to re-establish themselves within the gut.

Case Study:

A 23-year-old woman came to me with diarrhea, nausea, vomiting, and constant abdominal pain. Her stool culture grew Yersinia enterocolitica, a bacteria related to the Bubonic plague. She took two weeks of ciprofloxacin, a strong antibiotic, and recovered completely. We combined this with an elimination diet. Her acne and digestive issues almost completely resolved within two months.

Many people have negative emotional relationships with their food. With all the distractions of modern life, few people are truly taking the time to relax and enjoy their food. They are shoveling it into their mouths and choking it down as fast as they can. This is an extremely unhealthy habit. The body needs to be in a relaxed state for hours each day. Many people are in a state of relaxation for just moments each day. These people inevitably become patients. Unless they change their lifestyle to incorporate time for rest, relaxation, and the enjoyment of food, music, friends, and family, they will not recover. These people frequently hop from practitioner to practitioner, from method to method, from gadget to gadget, diet to diet, without ever experiencing true healing. Their mindset and lifestyle are the problem.

Finally, a lack of proper nutrients can drive adverse reactions to foods. Patients who, for example, lack vital minerals like copper, zinc, magnesium, potassium, or calcium frequently complain of indigestion. They are usually diagnosed with irritable bowel syndrome, but often respond quickly to nutritional supplementation. Vitamins are also critical to proper digestion. Many patients have food sensitivities that resolve once they have corrected mineral or vitamin deficiencies.

Nutritional deficiencies have become a controversial topic. For example, most physicians recognize fish oil as an important component of a healthy diet.

But how much fish should we eat? How much fish oil do you need? How much does this vary from person to person based on their biochemical individuality? Patients are not being sold testing – they are being sold supplements. The result is that many people today are taking nutritional supplements, but without any idea of how much of any given supplement they actually need.

I routinely see patients with fish oil levels well over those associated with optimal health. I also see patients with low levels of other essential fatty acids, such as omega-6 fatty acids. I see toxic levels of zinc, copper, selenium, aluminum, mercury, and arsenic on a regular basis. I see deficiencies of amino acids, B-vitamins, and other essential nutrients as well. One of the challenges with minerals in particular is that minerals compete with one another. A high intake of copper can cause a zinc deficiency and vise-versa. The same is true of manganese and molybdenum. When patients first start to work with me, I recommend that they stop taking all supplements as tolerated – meaning, so long as they will not suffer acute withdrawal symptoms. Nutritional supplements must be guided by testing. They are powerful therapeutic interventions that must not be underestimated or dismissed as benign.

Restrictive diets also cause nutritional deficiencies. Folate is a deficiency I frequently diagnose in my practice. It is commonly said that green, leafy vegetables are a great source of folate, but the truth is that you have to eat excessive amounts of them to obtain high levels of folate in your diet. Legumes, particularly black beans, have a much higher density of folate. Without legumes, patients tend to develop folate deficiencies. This is not universally true, but generally true. Nuts, as another example, are our main source of arginine. Patients who do not eat nuts tend to develop low arginine levels. B-12 is primarily found in animal products, including seafood and dairy. Deficiencies are common in vegetarians and vegans. The result of nutritional deficiencies are chronic, complex diseases that are then managed by most doctors with drugs and surgeries. These drugs and surgeries are ineffective in truly healing the problem.

Modern academic medical centers take little interest in nutrition as a subject of clinical study. Sadly, they also take a backwards view of the topic in the few studies that they do undertake. There is little rigorous study of what optimal nutrition looks like coming out of academia. Patients are left wondering how much of this or that to take, and doctors do not know enough to advise them competently. The result is epidemics of disease that are entirely preventable and treatable.

All of this begins and ends with technology. Modern technology has allowed us to radically alter the food that we eat. We can eat whatever we want, whenever we want, laced with whatever food manufacturers think will make it last, taste, smell, look, sound, or feel better to the consumer. Those who eat a traditional diet, with minimal processing, tend to be healthier in all respects. This is not to dismiss the importance of the rest of the environment. If just one factor in your environment is unhealthy, it can drive your disease forward no matter what you do. For example, if your sleep is being disrupted by light, sound, or electromagnetic pollution, then no amount of drugs, surgeries, supplements, dieting, exercising, or meditation will cure what ails you.

Personal Care Products

I always hesitate when I am tempted to blame someone's personal care products as the source of their illness. People get emotionally attached to these products, but they are loaded with chemicals and even natural ingredients that can cause disease. We can develop allergies and sensitivities to things that we put on our skin, which may be mediated either by their action on the skin itself or through our airway. I find that patients are frequently sensitive to fragrances and scents, and may not even realize it.

What can you do about personal care product allergies and toxicities? Unfortunately, whether or not personal care products are "healthy" or "unhealthy" has become about whether or not they are "organic" or "natural." This misses the point almost entirely. There are several problems with just trusting a product as "healthy" based on labels like natural, organic, cruelty-free, non-GMO, soy-free, gluten-free, dairy-free, or fair trade, just to name a few.

For example, you may have a deficiency of omega-3's leading to dry skin. In this case, flax or walnut oil might be very therapeutic to your skin. But what if the flax or walnut oil has gone rancid and is loaded with free radicals? This is a common problem with omega-3 and 6 fatty acids, particularly when we refine them and put them into personal care products. Is a rancid oil that you are deficient in good for you, or bad for you? As another example, we can develop allergies to things that are nonetheless of extremely high quality. There is no reason that you can't have an allergy or skin sensitivity to organic ingredients. Poison ivy is a class example of a perfectly natural and organic product that, nonetheless, causes severe allergic reactions in some people. Frequently, these reactions defy our ability to detect with standard scientific methods. For example, a patient may report severe nausea and headaches when exposed to a specific fragrance, but we may never find any laboratory abnormalities that reflect this.

What are we to do about this? In difficult cases, I frequently ask patients to stop all personal care products for up to 72 hours. As painful as this is for some of them, it is sometimes instrumental in gaining clarity on what is actually making them sick. I always prefer and recommend very simple personal care products. The fewer ingredients, the better. "Natural" and "organic" do not always mean "better." They have largely at this point become meaningless tools of clever marketers. If you are going to use organic and natural products, do your homework on the company. Make sure they are actually walking the walk, not just talking the talk. This can be difficult to impossible in a world where a good-looking website is easy to make and companies we are buying from keep their operations all over the world, where we cannot directly observe what they are doing or how they are doing it.

Fortunately, I rarely find that personal care products are a significant problem for patients. They are typically bit players, rather than main actors, in causing their illness. Between air, water, food, and personal care products, we have covered all of the physical matter that you come into contact with on a daily basis. This is the "m" variable in Einstein's famous equation. Next, we will address the more complex and quixotic variable in his equation - energy, or "E," for short.

What Is Energy?

Before talking about energy, I think it is important to define what energy is. Matter is anything that has mass. Energy is everything else, and acts upon and within matter to produce change. Energy is neither created nor destroyed, merely transformed and transferred. The four fundamental forces of nature, the nuclear strong force, the nuclear weak force, the electromagnetic force, and gravity give rise to all of the energies that we are subject to in life. Each of these has distinct effects on our health, but only gravity and the electromagnetic force are directly relevant to your health and your day to day choices. You are already painfully aware of the effects of gravity - who hasn't fallen down and been hurt by this force? The entire body is organized to take advantage of gravity - food starts at the top of your body and flows down as it is transformed into waste.

Of the four fundamental forces, it is the electromagnetic force that has the most powerful, profound, and yet subtle effects on health. A few nanometers difference in the wavelength of light may make the difference between health and disease. All four fundamental forces can and do give rise to another form of energy that is important to your health - sound, which includes any physical vibration of matter.

Electromagnetism and Life

All life on earth depends upon the electromagnetic force. What is the electromagnetic force? What is so remarkable about this force is that it defies simple definition. Albert Einstein elucidated the strange nature of electromagnetism in his most important papers on physics. The electromagnetic force includes light, which itself exists along a spectrum from radiowaves (very low energy and not visible to our eyes) to visible light (the colors of the rainbow) to invisible ultraviolet light, and beyond, to dangerously powerful forms of light we call "ionizing radiation." The electromagnetic force also include electrical and magnetic fields and currents. For example, the electromagnetic force is responsible for flow of electrons within a wire that might run a lightbulb. The energy from the flow of electrons creates light, as well as a slight magnetic field around the electrical current. The same flow of electrons runs your washing machine, dryer, air conditioning, television, and cell phone. Likewise, light striking a solar panel generates an electrical current, the energy of which can then be stored and transmitted elsewhere.

This is not a book on physics - I include these details only to impress upon you that all of these phenomena are unified and interrelated. One of the reasons modern people are so sick is that they ignore the totality of the effects of these different forces and energies. Understanding them is central to achieving and maintaining good health.

We will discuss them in three categories - light, electromagnetic pollution, and sound.

Light

What is light? Light exists along a spectrum, known as the electromagnetic spectrum. Radio and microwave radiation are the lowest forms of electromagnetic energy. Infrared light is next, which we perceive as heat. Visible light comes next, with red being the lowest energy and blue or violet being the highest. Ultraviolet light comes next, and after that we get a variety of high-energy radiations like x-rays and gamma rays, which are very dangerous. The earth's atmosphere naturally filters out everything below infrared light and everything above ultraviolet type B light. Life on earth has a use for every single frequency of light that penetrates our atmosphere, from infrared to UV-B light. This has profound ramifications for our health and disease.

Light can create health and it can destroy it. Most people do not realize just how powerfully light shapes life. Light drives all of the cycles of nature. The day-night cycle is driven by the rotation of the earth around its axis. The seasons are driven by the tilting of the earth on its axis. Seasons of abundance are seasons of light. Seasons of scarcity are seasons of darkness.

What wakes us up in the morning? How do we go to sleep at night? How do polar bears know when to hibernate and when to come back out of hibernation? How do the elk or the wildebeest know when to migrate? Light is the answer. Light is a signal of abundance, while darkness is a signal of scarcity.

Humans used to migrate, and those who can afford to still do. We migrate up to cool mountain lakes in the summer, or down to the beach. We migrate back to the lowlands and southerly climes when winter returns. Temperature is just a function of the amount of sunlight reaching the earth's surface. Light shapes life and we depend upon it for many of our vital functions.

How do our bodies use and respond to light? Blue and green light wake us up in the morning and help to set our circadian rhythms. Red and infrared light help to tune our mitochondria to improve energy generation within our cells. Ultraviolet light helps to modulate our hormone levels and to create vitamin D. Light has powerful effects on health that I see in my practice on a daily basis.

Case Study:

A young woman came to me complaining of body aches and pains, abdominal pain and indigestion, and vertigo. An incidental complaint of hers was that her eyes burned and got tired late in the day or at night. Part of my prescription was that she remedy her light environment. She was to avoid artificial light at night, by wearing red-tinted glasses. She was to get some sunlight, especially in her eye, sometime during the day. The same day she implemented these changes, her eyes stopped burning. She had seen ophthalmologists for this problem in the past, yet had been given no advice on light. She no longer needs an ophthalmologist.

Modern lighting has had the red and infrared portions of the visible spectrum edited out. This has been done in the name of energy efficiency. The tragedy for human eyesight and longevity is that our bodies depend upon red and infrared light for optimal health. This is why ocular diseases are rapidly increasing in prevalence and severity. It is why kids need glasses more today than ever before in history.

We have also completely edited ultraviolet light out of life. Glass filters 99% of ultraviolet light. Most people spend 95% of their time indoors. The time we spend outside, little of our skin is in direct sunlight. The result is the modern epidemic of vitamin D deficiency, which in turn is fueling modern epidemics of cancer, cardiovascular disease, and mental and neurological illnesses. Time outside, in sunlight, is the answer for many modern health problems.

One of the great tragedies of modern medicine is the vilification of the sun. While it is true that the sun can cause photo-aging, or "light" aging of the skin, it is also vital to good health. In the Melanoma in Southern Sweden Trial (MISS), researchers found that the study participants who spent the least time in the sun had the same likelihood of death as those who spent the most time outside, but smoked.[128] This result suggests that spending time indoors is as bad for you as smoking. The logical response is not to spend excessive time outside, but to spend a moderate amount of time outside in bright sunlight. This ensures adequate production of vitamin D, alpha-MSH, and many other beneficial molecules.

Case Study:

A young woman who lived in the Upper Midwest came to see me for melasma. Melasma is a disease in which normal pigmentation of the skin is impaired. Patients develop pale patches of skin that they are embarrassed by. She wore sunglasses and worked in an office. Comprehensive nutritional testing revealed that she had multiple nutritional deficiencies related to the pathways responsible for skin pigmentation. With the right dietary changes and nutritional supplements, and prudent sun exposure each day (including without sunglasses), she began to see her melasma disappear. It is not uncommon for many skin issues to disappear for patients once they realize just how powerfully light is affecting their skin tone, texture, and quality.

128   Lindqvist, P. G., Epstein, E., Nielsen, K., Landin-Olsson, M., Ingvar, C., & Olsson, H. (2016). Avoidance of sun exposure as a risk factor for major causes of death: a competing risk analysis of the Melanoma in Southern Sweden cohort. Journal of internal medicine, 280(4), 375–387.

While we have vilified the sun, few people appreciate the hazards of indoor lighting and artificially lit screens. A hundred years ago, when lightbulbs were first invented, they had a warm, amber glow. The spectrum of light they emitted was similar to that of the sun. Today, we have light-emitting diodes (LED) and fluorescent (compact and otherwise) bulbs that emit a much harsher, 'cooler' spectrum of light. This might not seem like an important detail, but it has significant consequences for our health. The blue and green wavelengths of light wake us up, but they also are a stress on our eyes and skin. Red and infrared light provide a natural antidote to this stress. Sunlight contains the perfect balance of light from infrared to ultraviolet. It is the spectra of light we are best adapted to. When we are exposed to blue and green light at night, it disrupts our circadian rhythms. This results in poor sleep, poor regeneration of the body, and premature aging. This is why working at night is strongly linked to premature cancer,[129] heart disease,[130] dementia,[131] neurological disorders,[132] and mental illness.[133] Every system of the body depends upon proper circadian rhythms, and therefore no system is immune to the harmful effects of artificial light at night.

Today, people are constantly exposed to blue and green light via cell phones, tablets, computers, and indoor lights. It is easy to choose warmer, less harmful lights over brighter lights. In my practice, I have found that no amount of diet, exercise, drugs, or surgeries will fix a problem caused by an unhealthy light environment.

Case Study:

A young woman came to me complaining of severe headaches. She worked as a veterinary tech and was often in the operating room under harsh lights. She spent a lot of time at work on the computer entering data. She noticed that her headaches were worse at work. I recommended that she try red-tinted glasses, which soften the light from computer screens and artificial indoor lights. A few weeks later, her headaches were half as frequent and half as

129   Yang, W. S., Deng, Q., Fan, W. Y., Wang, W. Y., & Wang, X. (2014). Light exposure at night, sleep duration, melatonin, and breast cancer: a dose-response analysis of observational studies. European journal of cancer prevention : the official journal of the European Cancer Prevention Organisation (ECP), 23(4), 269–276.
130   Thomas Münzel, Omar Hahad, Andreas Daiber, The dark side of nocturnal light pollution. Outdoor light at night increases risk of coronary heart disease, European Heart Journal, Volume 42, Issue 8, 21 February 2021, Pages 831–834
131   Bokenberger, K., Sjölander, A., Dahl Aslan, A. K., Karlsson, I. K., Åkerstedt, T., & Pedersen, N. L. (2018). Shift work and risk of incident dementia: a study of two population-based cohorts. European journal of epidemiology, 33(10), 977–987.
132   Jin, Y., Hur, T. Y., & Hong, Y. (2017). Circadian Rhythm Disruption and Subsequent Neurological Disorders in Night-Shift Workers. Journal of lifestyle medicine, 7(2), 45–50.
133   Lee, A., Myung, S. K., Cho, J. J., Jung, Y. J., Yoon, J. L., & Kim, M. Y. (2017). Night Shift Work and Risk of Depression: Meta-analysis of Observational Studies. Journal of Korean medical science, 32(7), 1091–1096.

severe. She no longer needs to see me for her headaches.

Light is one of our most powerful tools to treat disease, yet most physicians are largely unaware of its potential to heal or to harm. The use of light to treat disease is one of the most important and exciting frontiers in medicine.

Non-Native Electromagnetic Radiation

Do cell phones cause cancer? This is one of the most controversial questions in modern science and medicine. It is the one most hotly debated when it comes to the question of the effects of electromagnetic radiation on the human body.

By non-native electromagnetic radiation, I refer to electromagnetic energies that are artificial or "non-native" to life on earth. What exactly does that mean? With modern technology, we produce enormous amounts of electromagnetic radiation that would otherwise not be present on earth anywhere, ever. Radio and microwaves from space are blocked by the atmosphere and levels on earth prior to the invention of the radio in the early 1900's were practically zero. Electrical and magnetic fields in nature are miniscule and restricted to fields within and around living organisms, or to the electromagnetic field generated by the earth itself (known as the Schumann Resonance). Modern technology has introduced enormous amounts of these artificial electromagnetic energies to our environment.

There can be no debate that the human body is an electromagnetic organism.[134] Every biochemical reaction within the body relies upon this force to progress, and the motion of fluids and currents around the body are mediated, at their most fundamental level, by the electromagnetic force. The question, since the invention of modern electricity and the radio, is whether or not these forces can impact our health.

Electromagnetic radiations include radiofrequency radiations, electrical fields, and magnetic fields. These fields are generated by modern consumer electronics. The magnitude of the field varies widely. The radio emitter in modern car keys, that starts the engine, does not register on even highly sensitive meters. Your cell phone, when calling or using wireless data, emits

---

134   Becker, Robert O., Gary Selden, and David Bichell. "The body electric: Electromagnetism and the foundation of life." (1985).

radiofrequency radiations that are many orders of magnitude higher than what is naturally present here on earth.

A 2011 study by Nora Volkow, MD, published in the Journal of the American Medical Association, showed that cell phone radiation can alter blood flow to the brain.[135] The clinical significance of this, the paper concludes, is uncertain. Many people use a cell phone for hours each day and have no manifestations of neurological or psychiatric disease. Yet the incidence of these diseases is increasing rapidly in our society. There are many other factors that may contribute to this – virtual interactions replacing in-person interactions, new toxins such as pesticides and herbicides in our food and water, air pollutants, and many more.

Epidemiological studies examining the question of safety of cell phones have shown mixed results. Some show increased rates of cancer, while others do not. In all of these studies, there are numerous confounding variables. For example, as people have adopted cell phones, they have also adopted wireless earbuds, wireless internet routers, smart appliances, wireless chargers, and bluetooth devices. Cell phones now make up just a component of the average person's exposure to these fields. Do electromagnetic fields and emissions harm humanity? Debate will continue until enough people have experienced the harms of these fields and emissions.

For me, this question became academic long ago. My patients made it clear to me that in many cases, medical problems disappeared following the removal of extraneous electromagnetic fields. They are not something that I address initially with any patient, because there are more important factors, but there have been many cases in which mitigating the electromagnetic radiations in the environment made the difference between success and failure.

Case Study:

A 45-year-old man developed severe high blood pressure. He was fit, ate a full diet, and had no other medical conditions. His blood pressure was, at one point, so severe that he was admitted to the hospital. He improved his diet and restricted his salt intake, but his blood pressure remained elevated. He ended up on three different blood pressure medications at maximum doses. He then moved into a new home. Over the following months, he was able to taper off of all his blood pressure medications and has had a normal blood pressure ever since. Upon discovering links between cardiovascular disease

---

135   Volkow ND, Tomasi D, Wang G, et al. Effects of Cell Phone Radiofrequency Signal Exposure on Brain Glucose Metabolism. JAMA. 2011;305(8):808–813.

and electromagnetic radiation, he realized that he had been sleeping over the inverter for his solar panels and next to a smart meter at his old home. He concluded that this must have been the cause of his high blood pressure, as nothing else had changed in his diet, lifestyle, environment, or mental state.

This case was actually not a patient of mine, but a colleague named Rob Brown, MD. Rob is a radiologist in Arizona. I interviewed him and Beverly Rubik, PhD, regarding a paper they submitted for publication on the similarities between exposure to fifth-generation cell technology (better known as 5G) radiation and COVID-19. Their paper points out that the pathology seen in severe COVID-19 is identical to that seen with severe exposure to 5G. 5G cell technology was launched in Spring of 2020, at exactly the same time as COVID-19. They clearly state – for the record – that they do not think 5G causes COVID-19, but rather that 5G contributes to morbidity and mortality. Rob even got the COVID-19 vaccine when it came out. None of us believe that 5G alone can explain COVID-19, though we have been mischaracterized as saying that.

This theory has been viciously attacked in the mainstream media and mainstream academia. For some reason, the advocates of unrestricted 5G use do not want to do simple safety studies comparing morbidity and mortality between populations who are exposed at different levels to 5G. I find this remarkable, because it would be as simple as allowing one city to roll out 5G, while another delays the roll out of 5G. I believe that the industry, which stands to make untold profits from this new cell technology, is putting profits ahead of human health and safety. This is certainly the historical precedent that they have set.

Case Study:

A 48-year-old woman came to me with intractable migraine headaches. She initially responded to nutritional interventions, but eventually her improvement stalled. After about four months of working together, she purchased meters to detect electromagnetic fields in her home and started remediating them. It took two months for the electricians to rewire the home and reduce her exposures substantially, but once she had done so, her headaches all but disappeared. She had lived with them for decades. She never imagined she would gain such control over them as she has now.

People often ask me how much electromagnetic radiation they should allow into their lives. Healthy people can withstand a great deal of exposure, but the frail and chronically ill seem to be more susceptible. Nicola Tesla said, "If you want to understand the secrets of the universe, think in terms of energy, frequency, and vibration." I have been struck by how quixotic reactions to electromagnetic frequencies can be. I have seen eczema break out on the dominant hand, and switch to the non-dominant hand if the person starts to use their cell phone in the non-dominant hand. One person may be stricken by headaches when they put in wireless earbuds, but another will feel no difference at all. One person may develop tinnitus from a specific wireless router, while another may experience no symptoms. I do not know and cannot predict how changing the electromagnetic radiations within your environment will affect you. I can only testify to the fact that it has changed the lives of my patients for the better. I look for significant electromagnetic pollution in every difficult or treatment resistant case that I encounter for this reason.

Sound and Vibration

People think of sound and vibration as harmless, but the truth is that sound and vibration can have negative health effects. They are perhaps the most overlooked factor in disease, despite the fact that the first literature on noise pollution appeared decades ago.[136] We know that noise pollution from trains, highways, airports, and industrial activities cause premature aging.[137] This is an insidious process. Sound waves exert a physical force upon the body, to which the body responds by altering blood flow, autonomic function, and growth and tissue remodeling. Sound waves are increasingly being studied for their medicinal properties, with the hope that the right frequencies will help us to heal disease tissue.

Sound can also be a chronic stress. We know that excessive sound degrades sleep quality. This degradation of sleep quality can cause a cascade of effects. If you do not get high-quality sleep, your body cannot adequately regenerate. Premature aging is the result.

Sound also has profound emotional power over us. We come to associate songs with certain people, places, and times. Music can therefore have powerful effects on our mental state, and through it, the rest of our health. Listening to sad music constantly can produce sadness.[138] Listening to happy, upbeat music all the time has the opposite effect. If you ask people what kind

---

136   Smith, L. K. "Noise as a Pollutant." Canadian Journal of Public Health/Revue Canadienne de Sante'e Publique 61, no. 6 (1970): 475-480.
137   Jariwala, Hiral J., Huma S. Syed, Minarva J. Pandya, and Yogesh M. Gajera. "Noise Pollution & Human Health: A Review." Indoor Built Environ (2017): 1-4.
138   Garrido, Sandra, and Emery Schubert. "Music and people with tendencies to depression." Music Perception: An Interdisciplinary Journal 32, no. 4 (2015): 313-321.

of music they listen to, you can find out what their personality is, and from there you can deduce where they like to spend time, what their friends are like, and what they tend to do for fun – if they have fun at all.

We are facing increasing amounts of noise pollution due to over-crowded cities, expanding road systems, and even home appliances that emit a certain amount of background noise. The toll on our health is difficult to even estimate, but it is real. I counsel my patients about sound pollution in every case.

Energy moves and animates life. Most physicians are still too focused on the "matter" that shapes their patient's lives - their food in particular. Energy is just as if not more important than matter to good health. I have seen so many patients languish in disease under the care of physicians who only paid attention to their physical body. Doctors are the product of their training, and our training focuses on the material world to the exclusion of energy and energy medicine. Fortunately, doctors are starting to pay more and more attention to energy, but it is still not enough. There is so much to do to optimize the energy of your environment for your health and well-being.

Having a healthy environment, in terms of both matter and energy, is not enough for good health. Paradoxically, we also need stress, and there are unique stressors associated with each element of our environment. Stress is what the government and public health authorities are trying desperately to shield people from, and this is why their recommendations are so disastrous to the health of the individual and the public at large. Without stress, we become soft, weak, and susceptible to diseases of all kinds. In the next chapter, we will explore how the body responds to stress to become resilient.

7. Survival of the Stressed

How Stress Holds Us Up and Gradually Tears Us Down

"Walking is a man's best medicine."

- Hippocrates

People today are fond of vilifying stress. Stress is on the cover of every magazine and the front page of every website as the cause of all disease. This is ridiculous. Life organizes itself around stress, and stress is therefore indispensable to life.

The human body is organized to take advantage of stress within the environment. Your bones remodel based on the stresses you place upon them.[139] Exercise, which tones and strengthens the heart and vascular system, does so by stressing them. Mental exercise sharpens the mind and helps to prevent diseases like dementia. Every kind of stress we can encounter in nature can be used to create resilience and reverse disease. This is why it is so dangerous for public health authorities to shield people from stress.

Health depends upon stress. When you avoid stress, all of your faculties and strengths atrophy. Your muscles shrink and wither away. Your endurance and cardiovascular fitness decline. Your mental faculties slip away. Your bones weaken. Every system in your body needs stress to remain healthy.

Why, then, do people complain about stress?

There are two kinds of stress – eustress and distress. Eustress is stress that our bodies respond to positively, by becoming stronger. Distress is stress that has overwhelmed our capacity to respond to it. This is the difference between swimming and drowning, exercise and punishment, recreation and self-destruction.

---

139   Becker, Robert O., Gary Selden, and David Bichell. "The body electric: Electromagnetism and the foundation of life." (1985).

Stress must be balanced against the body's resources. The more you exercise, the more food you must consume to sustain that exercise. If you want to put on muscle in response to exercise, you have to eat more food, otherwise your body will start to break down muscle for fuel. Every nutrient the body requires comes in varying quantities in the food that you eat. This means that small changes to what you eat can lead to massive changes in your nutritional status.

We come to hate those who cause us or threaten us with distress. You don't force people to be uncomfortable – this is basic human decency. Eustress, however, is exactly what coaches, trainers, doctors, teachers, and parents push us into. We come to love these people, because they make us stronger. We have a natural desire for our stress to be of our choosing – we hate those who force either eustress or distress upon us. This is only natural. These people are forcing us to spend resources that we may not have, in order to deal with those stresses. We carefully balance our resources against the stresses we must meet in life, because failure means death.

Mismanaged stress is the cause of so much modern disease. People do not understand how to balance stress in their lives. This is why they have bad backs and joints from excessive exercise, skin cancers from excessive sunburning, or excess body fat or elevated blood sugar despite eating a prudent diet.

We are well-adapted to natural stresses. This is why so many of the forces of nature are, while also dangerous to us, indispensable to our health. Cold-stress protects us from gaining weight and developing elevated blood glucose levels.[140] Heat-stress prevents cardiovascular disease (sauna).[141] Holding your breath (diving) improves your overall cardiovascular fitness, protecting you from a wide array of diseases. Every aspect of our environment can become a stressor, so managing our stressors is a key to good health and longevity.

To be truly free, we need to be able to meet and endure stress. Otherwise, we become dependent upon others. Distress will break us down, and in our effort to minimize it, we have unwittingly grown soft, weak, and, as a result, sick. Big Food, Big Tech, and Big Pharma want it this way. Hippocrates said, "the greatest medicine of all is teaching people how not to need it." This requires the proper application of eustress. Americans today are struggling with premature illness and death, because they do not understand the vital nature of stress. They are distracted by and addicted to cheap junk food and digital

140   Remie, C., et al. (2021). Metabolic responses to mild cold acclimation in type 2 diabetes patients. Nature communications, 12(1), 1516.
141   Laukkanen, T., Kunutsor, S. K., Khan, H., Willeit, P., Zaccardi, F., & Laukkanen, J. A. (2018). Sauna bathing is associated with reduced cardiovascular mortality and improves risk prediction in men and women: a prospective cohort study. BMC medicine, 16(1), 219.

entertainment which keep them on the couch and out of the stresses of nature. They are then doomed to dependency upon pharmaceuticals. This is why I describe Big Food, Big Tech, and Big Pharma as parasites. They are sucking this country dry of its health and wealth with slavery 2.0.

While natural stressors can help us achieve greater health and well-being, the stresses of modern technology are a grave threat to our well-being. Americans fail to recognize the significance of this threat, largely because government and industry collude to fool them into thinking that modern technology is harmless and beneficial to society. The key to maintaining control over the American people is keeping them in the dark about the vital nature of stress to their health and well-being. This chapter is about dispelling these illusions, to explain exactly how to use stress to gain your freedom from this system.

Stress Matters

Today, the word "stress" conjures images of angry bosses, looming work deadlines, or interpersonal drama. Historically, our greatest stressors have been material. The essentials of life - air, water, and food - are what our ancestors "stressed" over. You can survive a few minutes without air, a few days without water, and a few weeks without food. Air, water, and food are the material concerns that are vital to life. Their absence can kill, but it can also strengthen us. This is the key to why practices like free-diving, breath-holding, exercise, sauna, and fasting can make us stronger and healthier, despite the fact that they are, by definition, stressful.

Modern doctors and public health authorities ignore the benefits of these practices, or at best pay lip service to them. People need these stresses in order to be healthy. If the average American were to embrace these practices and make them a part of their daily routine, the world would be a very, very different place. We would be a far healthier and more robust people. Sadly, our politicians have no incentive to make us so, when making us comfortable is the tried and true strategy to earn votes for re-election.

How does stress make us stronger? The answer is in how our bodies adapt to it. One of our most potent stresses is lack of air, and specifically a state that we call hypoxic hypercarbia.

Hypoxic, Hypercarbic Respiratory Training

The air you breathe is composed of oxygen, carbon dioxide, nitrogen, trace gasses (too numerous to mention), volatile organic compounds, and particulate matter. Each of these can act as stressors on your system, and each can be turned to your advantage (eustress) or disadvantage (distress).

The oxygen you depend upon for life is just as much a stress as it is a necessity. Too much oxygen will cause excessive oxidative stress. This is the biological equivalent of rust. It is associated with virtually all chronic diseases. The regulation of oxygen utilization and distribution throughout the body is vital to life. When we exercise, part of the benefit is the stress of alternating lack of oxygen (due to consumption by muscles) and part is due to the compensatory increase in blood flow to the muscle in question.

It only takes a few minutes without oxygen (asphyxia) for the cells of the brain to suffer irrevocable damage, and for the patient to die. Yet the careful lowering of oxygen tensions by exercise or breath-holding exert powerful effects on our physiology that can provide us with tangible physical advantages and likely longevity.[142]

Carbon dioxide plays an unappreciated role in your breathing. Most people think that when they are "out of breath," they are out of oxygen. You can confirm that this is not the case just by checking your oxygen levels with a pulse oximeter that you can buy at any drug store. Carbon dioxide is the primary stimulus to the human brain to breathe. We experience elevated levels of carbon dioxide as "stressful." This stress has remarkable health benefits that are only now being popularized the way they deserve to be. Carbon dioxide not only stimulates you to breathe, it opens your blood vessels, allowing blood to flow, it causes oxygen to be off-loaded from hemoglobin so that it can be consumed by your cells. You might look at the state of hyperventilation (low carbon dioxide) as actually being a state of oxygen deprivation. The oxygen that the body does have will not be off-loaded to tissues, due to the low carbon dioxide level. To make matters worse, the low carbon dioxide levels will leave blood vessels abnormally tight, making it difficult for blood to flow around the body to supply your organs and tissues. This makes hypoxic, hypercarbic respiratory training an incredible practice to building health and resilience.

What happens when you hold your breath? Carbon dioxide begins to accumulate. Oxygen levels eventually drop. The result is that your body begins to acclimate to a higher level of carbon dioxide and a lower level of oxygen. You become accustomed to operating at this extreme, and will be able to do

142   Fahrizal, Dani, and Totok Budi Santoso. "The Effect of Buteyko Breathing Technique in Improving Cardiorespiratory Endurance." Proceedings of ISETH 2017 (The 3rd International Conference on Science, Technology, and Humanity), 2017.

so more and more comfortably. This kind of breath training confers greater endurance, improved cognition, and higher levels of maximal exertion.

The body must have the time and resources, however, to adapt to this stress. It must have the necessary nutrients to generate new red blood cells, to create new cellular machinery to cope with higher levels of carbon dioxide and lower levels of oxygen. These adaptations can then allow one to withstand longer and longer periods of absolute deprivation from oxygen.

Someone who routinely practices breath holding can withstand the dangers of oxygen deprivation far better than one who never does. This is a level of freedom, of being able to do and endure more, that can only be gained with the proper application of stress – eustress versus distress. This is the freedom enjoyed by free divers.

Hyperventilation syndrome is a diagnosis that has unfortunately been forgotten by most modern doctors. This was a syndrome clearly described and recognized by physicians just a few generations ago.[143] They recognized that patients who breathed too many times per minute had poor health. When I first learned this, I immediately recognized how profoundly important it was. My sickest patients always had higher breathing rates (respiratory rates). Higher respiratory rates went hand in hand with higher heart rates and blood pressure abnormalities. Hyperventilation is both a cause of and a result of disease. This is one reason clinicians have fallen into the mistake of dismissing it as clinically irrelevant.

What are the manifestations of hyperventilation syndrome? The list is long and includes many complaints for which Big Pharma now has a wide array of drugs. I address breathing mechanics with every patient in my practice because of how great an impact it has on their overall health. Big Pharma has engineered a literature focused on drugs, when what we really need to do is to fix the patient's breathing mechanics.

The Dangers of Artificially Filtered Air

Beyond oxygen and carbon dioxide, there are other stressors in the air that we seem to depend upon for good health. For example, in nature we are exposed to mold spores, botanical fragrances, dust, airborne bacteria, viruses, and fungi. Modern air filtration systems have drastically reduced our exposure to these, while increasing our exposure to indoor pollutants like pet dander and

---

143   Lewis, R. A., and J. B. Howell. "Definition of the hyperventilation syndrome." Bulletin européen de physiopathologie respiratoire 22, no. 2 (1986): 201-205.

dust mites. The result is an epidemic of allergies to all airborne allergens. We do not so much need to clean up our air as we need to return it to its natural state. I find it ironic that not long ago we were unable to escape things like pollen and mold spores, yet allergies to these things were extremely rare. This is the essence of the Hygiene Hypothesis mentioned earlier. When we alter our relationship with microbes, we inadvertently create allergic and autoimmune diseases. Breath-holding and fresh air are two of our most important stressors for this reason, and this is why spending time outside and under the water are two things I strongly recommend to many of my patients. It is also why I work with them on their breathing mechanics, long before ever telling them to get into the water.

Over-Hydration, Dehydration, Heat, and Cold Exposure

Most people do not think of water as a "stressor," but water is the mediator of many of the most important and beneficial stresses of life. Our bodies must balance electrolytes and water carefully because abnormalities of either can be fatal. We lose water and electrolytes in our urine and sweat. Electrolytes, perhaps better called minerals, must be balanced between deficiency and excess. Low levels of any electrolyte can be fatal, but so can excessive levels. Low or high levels of electrolytes are therefore stresses that our bodies can adapt to. We are no longer using these stresses properly to remain healthy, and the result is that we have epidemics of diseases linked to electrolyte and water imbalances, like high blood pressure, low blood pressure, cardiovascular disease, and stroke.[144]

Historically, we have struggled to maintain adequate levels of salt (sodium and other electrolytes) compared to water. Sweating, cold-exposure, and any form of exercise will waste electrolytes and water. This is why salt has always been a valuable commodity. It is why we like the taste of salt. It is an excellent source of minerals that we need, and that we are particularly prone to losing with heat or strenuous exercise.

The stress of exercise,[145] of sauna (or heat in general),[146] or of cold exposure[147] all result in changes in water and electrolyte balance within our bodies. This stress is beneficial in moderation, but dangerous in excess. As we have moved away from the stresses of heat, cold, and exercise, we have seen

---

144   Karppanen, Heikki. "Minerals and blood pressure." Annals of medicine 23, no. 3 (1991): 299-305.
145   Jennings, G. L., G. Deakin, E. Dewar, E. Laufer, and L. Nelson. "Exercise, cardiovascular disease and blood pressure." Clinical and Experimental Hypertension. Part A: Theory and Practice 11, no. 5-6 (1989): 1035-1052.
146   Nguyen, Yen, Nauman Naseer, and William H. Frishman. "Sauna as a therapeutic option for cardiovascular disease." Cardiology in review 12, no. 6 (2004): 321-324.
147   Lesna, I. Kralova, J. Rychlikova, L. Vavrova, and S. Vybiral. "Could human cold adaptation decrease the risk of cardiovascular disease?." Journal of thermal biology 52 (2015): 192-198.

increases in many chronic diseases.

Today, we are eating more and more salt and phosphorus, consuming less water, and spending less and less time exercising, sweating, or enduring cold temperatures. Modern diets tend to be low in potassium, magnesium, and calcium (among other trace elements) due to food processing and a shift toward more animal foods over plant foods. Animal foods tend to be lower in these elements, while plant foods tend to be richer. Food is our major source of minerals, but water is a significant contributor to overall mineral status. Water in nature contains a certain amount of minerals, typically potassium, calcium, and magnesium, and levels of these elements in our water are linked to better health.[148] Today, our most expensive spring waters are still rich in these minerals – their value is obvious to our palates. Tap water and filtered water are low in these minerals. The result is an epidemic of diseases linked to mineral and water imbalances. Sedentary Americans are dying in droves because they have ruined their healthy, historical relationship with water and electrolytes.

This is why sauna, exercise, and cold therapy are stresses that I discuss with every patient, in addition to ensuring a diet rich in potassium, magnesium, and calcium. We have abandoned these practices to our detriment. These are stresses that we need to achieve optimal health. America's public health establishment ignores the vital nature of water and salt balance, and therefore stress, to our health.

I have found that some people are actually over-hydrated. These people are generally drinking large quantities of filtered water, and they may restrict salt as well. They do not show up in the emergency room with critically low salt levels. Instead, they show up in my clinic complaining of fatigue, low blood pressure, depression, anxiety, poor sleep, and more symptoms and signs of mineral deficiency. You can exhaust your body's minerals with too much water, effectively diluting your body to the point of impairing its function. These patients need salt, a mineral-rich diet, and a careful selection of mineral waters that will not deplete them of minerals.

The stress of exercise, sauna, and cold all deplete us of salt, while the ingestion of natural mineral waters repletes us with calcium, magnesium, potassium, and other vital trace elements. The removal of these stresses has been a major mistake of modernity.

---

148   Catling, Louise A., Ibrahim Abubakar, Iain R. Lake, Louise Swift, and Paul R. Hunter. "A systematic review of analytical observational studies investigating the association between cardiovascular disease and drinking water hardness." Journal of water and health 6, no. 4 (2008): 433-442.

Fasting, Feeding, and the Stresses of Eating

Most people do not associate stress with eating, but what we eat, how much we eat, and when we eat can all cause "stress." Fasting can be looked at as a stress. When we deprive the body of nutrition, we trigger many metabolic pathways that are associated with longevity. How we process our food will alter how it stresses us. When we process food, we often remove hard, fibrous elements that are hard to chew. We then chew less, which triggers the production of less saliva and provides less fiber to the rest of the digestive tract. We also tend to remove fats and oils from food that will spoil. These include omega-6 and omega-3 fatty acids, which are vital to life. If we leave fats and oils in food, but do not store them properly, they can go rancid. All of this means that different foods can exert different forms of stress upon our bodies, and that stress depends upon how we process and store those foods.

Big Food has been able to achieve absurdly low prices for their products by doing everything to remove ingredients that may spoil or that people find unpalatable. We have removed fiber and natural fats from our food. Along with the fiber and fat, we have also removed vitamins and minerals that are essential to good health through excessive processing. Certain fats spoil less easily than others, and Big Food adds these to their products to improve the taste. The result is that Americans now over-consume (on average) saturated fats and certain omega-6 fats, and these have been implicated in the rise of cancers, cardiovascular diseases, and metabolic diseases like diabetes over the past several decades. Americans have never consumed so little omega-3 fats, which are vital to a healthy metabolism and immune system.

People like palatable food, and they like to eat a lot of it, often. This is a stress in and of itself. Putting two, three, four, or even five thousand calories into the body, as many people do, can create disease. Caloric restriction is one of the greatest stressors that can improve longevity that has ever been discovered. In general, the more fiber a food contains, the fewer calories it contains and the more minerals and vitamins it has. A stress as seemingly unremarkable as moving your jaw has far greater implications for your health and Big Food wants you to know. This is one reason why so many studies show that higher intake of fruits, vegetables, and nuts show improvements in health and metabolism. Few people need to eat more than 2,000 calories. People between 5 feet and 6 feet tall generally need only 1200 to 1800 calories. Fasting (caloric restriction) and fibrous foods are stresses that Americans need. Big Food and Big Pharma stand to lose a fortune if these stressors return to the American way of life.

People forget the stress involved in obtaining and preparing food. These stresses cannot be ignored. Think of how much work is required to fashion tools, such as bows, let alone guns, to bring down wild game. Think of how much work it takes to cut wheat (or other grains) with a scythe, to winnow the wheat from the chaff, to grind the wheat into flour, and then to make bread out of it. This takes enormous effort. Americans today are more sedentary than ever, and this includes how they obtain their food. We can now punch a few buttons on a phone and have food delivered to our homes. How much effort does it take to walk from the couch to the front door to take food from the delivery driver?

People do not think about stress when they think about food, but they should. Public health agencies are wasting their time trying to tax foods like soda, when they should be educating the public about the benefits of whole, natural foods and fasting. They ignore the corruption of the government by Big Food. If we were to eliminate subsidies to Big Food, American food would become more nutritious overnight. Junk food and soda would become expensive, while healthy foods would remain stable in price. This would shift consumption to healthier food, creating a healthier nation. Infectious diseases do not prey upon the well-nourished, but the malnourished. America's malnourishment is the fault of Big Food, and creates the market for Big Pharma's snake oils. Food should not just be about comfort and convenience, it should be about stressors like fasting and fiber.

Energy and Stress

Most people do not realize that "energy" can be a stress. A jet engine creates vibrations that create sounds and shockwaves that stress your hearing and therefore your brain. Light striking your retina creates a change in the rods and cones of the retina, sending an electrical signal to your brain that is, literally, a "stress." This is why when people are "stressed" they like to lie down in a dark, quiet room alone, or with someone who they find comforting.

Energetic stressors modulate our physiology to make us stronger and more resilient. Ultraviolet light is a stress that can burn our skin, but it also makes vitamin D, which is a vital nutrient. Blue light wakes us up in the morning, sets our circadian rhythms, and allows us to see our physical environment, but it is also a stress that can trigger oxidation and lipid peroxidation in our skin, which are associated with many skin diseases and disorders, including skin cancer. Sound can soothe and calm us, but it can also make us extremely anxious (just go listen to a horror movie soundtrack for confirmation of this).

Energetic stress is one of the key ingredients to living a healthy life, whether we are talking about the stress caused by exposure to visible light from your television, invisible microwaves from your cell phone, or sound from your air conditioning unit.

Let There Be Light: The Stress of Infrared, Visible, and Ultraviolet Light

Light is one of the most important sources of stress in nature. When light hits your skin or your eye, its energy is transformed in many ways. This is how light regulates your circadian rhythms and your skin color. Each of the wavelengths of light can act as a stress, but each of these wavelengths has critical functions for our health and well-being.

Every action of light upon the body qualifies as a stress. Light is therefore one of the greatest stressors that we face in the environment, and this makes it one of the greatest forces that your body can use to create and maintain health and vitality. Ultraviolet light is essential to production of vitamin D, endorphins, enkephalins, and endocannabinoids, which regulate our nervous and immune systems. Blue and green light stimulate the production of hormones and neurotransmitters, by their action upon the eye. The quantity of these signaling molecules that our bodies produce is directly proportional to the amount of light that hits our eyes. Red and infrared light stimulates energy production and generates heat. Any of these in excess can be dangerous.

"The dose makes the poison," as Paracelsus said. Too much ultraviolet light will create a nasty sunburn, which can eventually become skin cancer. It can also exhaust you. Many people notice that they cannot stand much time in the sun – it is tiring. It is stressful, even if we enjoy it. Yet there are many health benefits to this stress. I have noticed over my career that the unhealthiest Americans often spend little if any time in the sun. They are extremely pale. They also fail to eat colorful foods. One of the most common antioxidants in vegetables, beta-carotene, is orange. It can be broken down into vitamin A. If you over-consume it, it will deposit in your skin and turn you orange. Colorful molecules like beta-carotene are used by the body to neutralize the stress of free radicals, which are generated by ultraviolet light. This is why sun exposure actually reduces your risk of death overall.[149] This flies in the face of the standard medical advice to wear sunscreen and avoid sun exposure. How much ultraviolet light we can withstand depends upon many factors. Public health officials and experts are ignorant of the complexity of our relationship

149   Lindqvist P. G. (2018). The Winding Path Towards an Inverse Relationship Between Sun Exposure and All-cause Mortality. Anticancer research, 38(2), 1173–1178.

with ultraviolet light, and so their advice is to "wear sunscreen". This accounts for much of the chronic disease Americans are currently struggling with.

Blue and green light may not "burn" us per se, but they are still a stress that can overwhelm our bodies. Emerging research shows that these wavelengths of light increase levels of lipid peroxides in the skin[150] and increase the formation of reactive oxygen species.[151] These lipid peroxides can give rise to cancers. This likely explains why, as we have moved indoors and out of the sun, we have actually seen an increase in skin cancer. These wavelengths also drive our circadian rhythms. During the day, blue and green light wake us up and get us moving, but at night, blue and green light prevent us from releasing melatonin and entering deep, restful sleep. This is why, in an age of smartphones, tablets, computers, and wireless internet, we are faced with epidemics of sleep disorders. Blue and green light are vital to our minds, moods, and energy levels, and this is why light therapy for seasonal affective disorder always includes these wavelengths. Public health officials do not understand how blue and green light act as stressors, and why they are important to good health. They are instead advocating for public health measures that make hospitals, doctors, and drug companies obscene profits, while the average person has little if any real understanding of how light affects their health. We cannot live well without blue and green light. They are stressors that we need, but only in the proper time, place and balance. That time and place is the daytime, and they must be balanced by the other wavelengths of light we receive from the sun.

Red and infrared light can improve cellular energy production.[152] They can also heat your body, causing what we call heat stress. We already discussed the health benefits of sauna in the previous section on Water, but it is light that fundamentally imparts energy and therefore heat to water. This is why sauna is so strongly recommended by doctors of all kinds and in all specialties.

Light is a stress. Each wavelength causes stress within our bodies, to which we must respond by creating and releasing different chemicals. Without light, we become sick and die young. With excessive light, or with the wrong wavelengths at the wrong time (blue and green light at night), we can disrupt natural circadian rhythms and create disease. This is why closing parks and telling people to stay indoors and out of sunlight is moronic from a public health perspective. It deprives people of vitamin D, visible light (particularly

150   Ayaka, Y., et al. (2015). Blue light irradiation-induced oxidative stress in vivo via ROS generation in rat gingival tissue, Journal of Photochemistry and Photobiology B: Biology, 151,
151   Dong, K., Goyarts, E., Pelle, E., Trivero, J., Pernodet, N. (2019). Blue Light disrupts the circadian rhythm and create damage in skin cells. International Journal of Cosmetic Science. 41.
152   de Freitas, L. F., & Hamblin, M. R. (2016). Proposed Mechanisms of Photobiomodulation or Low-Level Light Therapy. IEEE journal of selected topics in quantum electronics : a publication of the IEEE Lasers and Electro-optics Society, 22(3), 7000417.

blue and green), red, and infrared light. As if that were not bad enough, it drives people indoors, where they bathe themselves with fake light that keeps them up all night. This undermines public health, rather than preserving it.

Light is a vital stressor for your health. Yet we hear nothing about it from public health authorities and doctors. They are busy prescribing and coercing people into the Big Pharma model of medicine. Ignoring the therapeutic and preventive value of light is one of the greatest failings of America's public health establishment.

Electromagnetic Radiation: An Unseen Force for Health and Wellness

Your body runs on the electromagnetic force. Pressure on your bones (from lifting weight) generates electrical current that causes bones to increase their strength and density. Electric currents mediate neurotransmission, heart function, blood flow, and the flow of ions into and out of cells. No element of your physiology goes unaffected by the electromagnetic force. Even the pineal gland that is responsible for the release of melatonin at night exhibits piezoelectric properties, generating current when small amounts of pressure are applied.

The electromagnetic force is integral to our stress response. When you see a threat, it is light that activates the photoreceptors in your retina, causing them to send an electrical signal to the rest of your brain. These signals are conducted down the sympathetic chain to the adrenal cortex, where they trigger the release of cortisol and catecholamines. The same nerves conduct these signals to your heart, where they cause the heart to beat faster and blood vessels to shift blood flow to your muscles in preparation for meeting the threat. Our stress response is electromagnetic in nature.

All of this is mediated by the electromagnetic force. This force surrounds us. The greatest electromagnetic field on earth is generated by the planet itself. This field resonates at what is called the Schumann Resonance. The earth's surface is constantly being charged by lightning that tends to fall most around the equator. These electrons can in fact be absorbed by living creatures when they make contact with the earth itself.[153] We call this "earthing" and it is one of the simplest and most effective ways to help people restore their health. To be in touch with the earth, we have to be connected by a conductive material. This has given rise to the development of "earthing shoes". Bare feet are arguably

153   Sinatra, S. T., Oschman, J. L., Chevalier, G., & Sinatra, D. (2017). Electric Nutrition: The Surprising Health and Healing Benefits of Biological Grounding (Earthing). Alternative therapies in health and medicine, 23(5), 8–16.

superior to earthing shoes, but are not practical in many situations.

When we are outside, connected to the earth's electromagnetic force, we are surrounded by stresses that build our strength and resilience. We may be walking, running, hiking, climbing, swimming, or diving. We are in natural sunlight and fresh air. We are surrounded by the sounds of nature. Each of these has therapeutic effects.

We are now surrounded by artificial electromagnetic fields, generated by modern electronics. These fields have subtle, but observable effects on our bodies and nervous systems. While many are quick to point out the negative health effects of these fields, it is just as important to note that all of our stress responses are mediated by the electromagnetic force. Every stress we can expose ourselves to has electromagnetic effects upon our bodies. The electromagnetic force holds incredible promise for future therapeutics and diagnostics for this reason.

Public health officials have no concept of how the electromagnetic force affects us. They have used quarantines and lockdowns to push people indoors, away from the natural stress of the earth's electromagnetic field, and into artificial fields that can cause harm. Reconnecting to the earth's electromagnetic field, and disconnecting from artificial fields, holds great promise for improving public health.

Sound and Vibration: How They Can Heal Us and Make Us Stronger

Sound has a profound effect on our bodies. Just think of how the words we hear can cause us to laugh or cry, and yet images alone rarely have this effect. A frown from someone you love cannot compare in the distress it causes to their outright verbal condemnation. Sound is a profound force for both healing, and for harm.

Sound is a mechanical vibration that, once absorbed by the body, is dissipated through its structures. This process within the ear is what we call hearing. Within the ear and the body, sound is conducted into the deepest parts of the brain, where it acts upon our emotional centers. We do not "think" about sound so much as we feel it. Neural projections from the ear reach every part of the brain, which means that what we hear can affect every aspect of how we think. Sound is, by definition, a stress.

How can the stress of sound make us stronger? First, we have always used percussion (striking the body in this case) as a therapeutic. Think about something as simple as patting someone on the back or slapping the back to help them cough up something that they had inhaled. Heavy bass is used in "pump up" songs to impart energy to the body, activating parts of the brain and therefore the body. How much athletic performance is thanks to the right music? Today, we have medical devices that percuss the body to induce tissue remodeling and regeneration. Sound is integral to their mechanism of action. The power of sound is being used to induce healing in the body with these devices.[154] Sound is a stress and it can be used to strengthen and tonify the body.

Singing and musical instruments are unique stressors that can be used to improve health.[155] Singing radically alters our breathing mechanics, and if done properly can improve our heart and lung capacity. Long exhales and inhales condition the body for larger breaths and strengthen the diaphragm. Changes in blood gas concentration, particularly elevations in carbon dioxide, condition the body for prolonged breath-holding and improved exercise capacity. Sound traveling through the body and increased intrathoracic pressure (from breathing out) can activate the vagus nerve. There is also a social aspect to singing – this dimension also strengthens our health. Perhaps this is part of why people who attend church are less likely to die.[156]

Sound is a stressor. Its power is multi-faceted and relates to every other aspect of our physiology. We ignore its power. Public health experts would rather close churches, where people gather to sing, than ask questions like, "how might singing improve public health?" This is why they have utterly failed to protect us from COVID, let alone protect the average American's health from the predatory practices of Big Pharma and Big Medicine.

The Dose Makes the Poison: How Much Stress Is Healthy?

How much stress should anyone undertake? This is unknowable. This is why we always allow people to choose how much stress to endure and to risk. I am constantly adjusting different therapeutic stresses in a patient's life to optimize their health. They may need more sauna or less sauna, more cold therapy or less cold therapy, more light or less light - and on and on. Despite

---

154   Yadollahpour, Ali, Jalilifar Mostafa, Rashidi Samaneh, and Rezaee Zohreh. "Ultrasound therapy for wound healing: A review of current techniques and mechanisms of action." J Pure Appl Microbiol 8 (2014): 4071-85.
155   Kang, Jing, Austin Scholp, and Jack J. Jiang. "A review of the physiological effects and mechanisms of singing." Journal of Voice 32, no. 4 (2018): 390-395.
156   Bruce, M.A., Martins, D., Duru, K., Beech, B.M., Sims, M., Harawa, N., Vargas, R., Kermah, D., Nicholas, S.B., Brown, A. and Norris, K.C., 2017. Church attendance, allostatic load and mortality in middle aged adults. PloS one, 12(5), p.e0177618.

the fact that my patients are frequently under a lot of stress, they rarely need treatment for acute illnesses, such as COVID-19, and this is because much of the stress they endure makes them stronger - not weaker. Understanding stress, and how it can make you stronger or weaker, depending on the timing, duration, and intensity of the exposure, can make or break your health. Public health authorities cannot simply "mandate" healthy stress, because it must be tailored to the individual. Likewise, there is an element of stress that is social. People often do not go to the gym or for a run because they enjoy it, they go because there is a social element to their stress. No matter where you go, the stresses that make us healthy are stresses that people prefer to enjoy together. This is why "social distancing" is a recipe for a sedentary, miserable, and unhealthy life.

This is why centralized, top-down attempts to create good health are doomed to failure. No one can tell you what stress you need in your life right now, in what duration or intensity to optimize your health. Likewise, they do not profit from recommending the stress that you need to be healthy. Growing your own food or buying it locally does not profit Big Food. Having local relationships and friendships does not profit Big Tech, except when those relationships are taken online. Healthy stressors like sunlight, exercise, and breath-holding do not enrich Big Pharma because they make you immune to the diseases that their drugs are prescribed to treat.

Those who would rule over us, mandating vaccines or masks as they see fit, will never mandate the kind of stress that people actually need to achieve optimal health. They already have enormous power to do exactly this, and they choose not to. This is why the notion that they care about human health is laughable.

8. Getting It All Wrong

How the Public Health Establishment Is Destroying America's Health

"I am more afraid of our own mistakes than of our enemies' designs."

- Pericles

Americans are told that their health is better for all the scientists and doctors that their tax dollars go to at institutions like the National Institutes of Health, the Centers for Disease Control, and the Food and Drug Administration. Nothing could be further from the truth. As we have seen over the course of 2020 and 2021, these "experts" are wrong more often than not. The models they used to justify shutting down society were wildly wrong. They have yet to demonstrate a clear clinical benefit from mask wearing or social distancing, among other measures that were shoved down the public's throat at the point of a gun over the past two years. As if being wrong were not bad enough, these experts lack even the decency to admit it. They are nothing short of delusional. Some of them are outright criminals who are a danger to society.

This is not new. It is, you may be surprised to learn, the norm. America's public health experts have been getting it wrong since they first decided that they were right generations ago. Their incompetence and arrogance has harmed countless Americans, and their hubris stands as an obstacle to true medical progress. The last two chapters have detailed why good health is a function of our choices, and those choices must include stress. This chapter will explain how the public health establishment is shielding the public from stress and in some cases actively poisoning them.

Air Quality Confusion: Why America's Respiratory Health Is Getting Worse

One of the few things public health officials have gotten right in the past century is cleaning up America's outdoor air quality. What they have neglected is America's indoor air quality. Americans now spend about 95% of their time indoors, which means that neglecting the quality of indoor air is tantamount to ignoring air quality entirely. We have cleaned up the air outside, but 95% of our time is spent breathing the air inside. Indoor air pollution is often hundreds or even thousands of times worse than outdoor air pollution,[157] yet public health experts do nothing to help Americans understand the importance of healthy indoor air.

The quality of your indoor air starts with your outdoor air quality, because outdoor air is brought into your home and then circulated through your heating and cooling system. While there are public health guidelines on outdoor air, there are none for indoor air. There are many factors that lead indoor air to be more polluted than outdoor air (it does not have to be), and there are many things that can be done to purify indoor air. You can use special filters, you can change the airflow in your home, you can replace carpet with hardwood floors, and you can have your ducts inspected and cleaned regularly. Public health experts ignore all of this, instead focusing only on outdoor air. They even use the "ozone" score to scare people into staying inside on hot, polluted days. The result is that Americans are given the illusion that they have healthy air to breathe, when in fact they have no idea how clean their indoor air is.

What is the result? Diseases of the organs that are exposed to the air — each of which "breathes" in its own way — are rapidly increasing in prevalence and severity. Children are now subject to epidemics of asthma and eczema, both of which are strongly linked to indoor air pollution.[158,159] These diseases often persist into adulthood, even to the point of crippling the patient. Rates of lung cancer are rising — why? We have virtually eliminated the vice of cigarette smoking, so smoking is not the answer. Rates of skin cancer are also rising, and it is likely due to our indoor lifestyles.[160] All of the top ten causes of death are related to lack of sun exposure, and therefore low vitamin D levels. Public health officials do not realize that their advice to keep people indoors for fear of outdoor air pollution is only worsening public health. They do not appreciate

157   Rudel, R. A., Camann, D. E., Spengler, J. D., Korn, L. R., & Brody, J. G. (2003). Phthalates, alkylphenols, pesticides, polybrominated diphenyl ethers, and other endocrine-disrupting compounds in indoor air and dust. Environmental science & technology, 37(20), 4543–4553.
158   Breysse, P. N., Diette, G. B., Matsui, E. C., Butz, A. M., Hansel, N. N., & McCormack, M. C. (2010). Indoor air pollution and asthma in children. Proceedings of the American Thoracic Society, 7(2), 102–106.
159   Kim, E. H., et al. (2015). Indoor air pollution aggravates symptoms of atopic dermatitis in children. PloS one, 10(3)
160   Merrill, S. J., Ashrafi, S., Subramanian, M., & Godar, D. E. (2015). Exponentially increasing incidences of cutaneous malignant melanoma in Europe correlate with low personal annual UV doses and suggests 2 major risk factors. Dermato-endocrinology, 7(1), e1004018.

how important air quality is, and so diseases of the lungs and respiratory tract continue to increase in prevalence and severity.

In contrast to this, the public health establishment has effectively reduced tobacco smoking by a remarkable degree. However, this was by no means a clear cut victory on the part of public health authorities over corporate interests. On the contrary, the industry played the regulatory agencies and public health establishment as long as possible to protect their profitability.[161] They fought what were essentially delaying actions against a controlled public health establishment, maintaining the appearance of good intentions. The credit that the government and public health authorities get for cleaning up America's smoking habit is rightly due to trial lawyers and citizen activists, who did the hard work of forcing government regulatory agencies to act. The same thing is happening right now with wireless radiation.

What about breathing mechanics? Dysfunctional breathing mechanics underlie a great deal of modern disease. Addressing this alone would provide a major improvement in public health. Does the public health establishment recommend or bother with this? They do nothing whatsoever to promote healthy breathing among the public. Their argument would be that we lack data to support this intervention. How much more data do they want? Might they, with all their public funding, be able to investigate the benefits of improved breathing mechanics? Of course they could, but they are too dim and uneducated to even realize that dysfunctional breathing mechanics are a problem. That is why most physicians, let alone patients, are ignorant of the importance of healthy breathing mechanics.

Allergies and asthma are on the rise despite improvements in our outdoor air quality, because of worsening indoor air quality, poor diet, sedentary, indoor lifestyles, and poor breathing mechanics. As if that were not enough, doctors are ignoring one of the best means of treating allergies - sublingual immunotherapy. Why? The FDA has not approved it for treatment of allergies and asthma, not because it does not work, but because no one will conduct definitive clinical trials proving that it works as well or better than injectable immunotherapy, let alone inhalers and other modern asthma medications.[162] Why can't anyone profit from it? Because no one can patent immunotherapy, since it is entirely natural. Why won't anyone put it through FDA approval? Because no one can patent it, and therefore no one can make a fortune on it. Most allergists today are ignoring it, because insurance will not reimburse for it. They are instead

161   Glantz, Stanton A., Richard Barnes, and Sharon Y. Eubanks. "Compromise or capitulation? US Food and Drug Administration jurisdiction over tobacco products." PLoS medicine 6, no. 7 (2009): e1000118.
162   Cox, L.S., Linnemann, D.L., Nolte, H., Weldon, D., Finegold, I. and Nelson, H.S., 2006. Sublingual immunotherapy: a comprehensive review. Journal of Allergy and Clinical Immunology, 117(5), pp.1021-1035.

offering patients injectable immunotherapy, which requires frequent office visits (multiple times a week) for injections that cause considerable swelling and discomfort at the injection site. Patients overwhelmingly prefer sublingual immunotherapy to injectable immunotherapy.[163] Why would we not use it? The answer is simply, "politics." Doctors and public health authorities are complicit in this. What is the result? Many patients avoid immunotherapy altogether, instead opting for inhalers and various other allergy and asthma medications. In allergic rhinitis and asthma, allergy immunotherapy has been found to provide a cost savings of up to 80% compared to drug treatments![164] In 2013, asthma alone cost Americans $81.9 billon.[165] Eighty percent of $81.9 billion is $65.5 billion. This is an ample incentive to maintain the costly and ineffective status quo, leaving Americans sick, weak, and broke. The failure of doctors and public health authorities to contain, let alone reduce, the cost of allergy treatments is truly a disgrace to our nation.

Many patients who seek out independent doctors like me see their respiratory problems resolve within a matter of months. Why? It is not a patentable medication or surgery. It is simply doing things a different way, first by focusing on the fundamentals of air quality and breathing mechanics, and second by improving the patient's diet and lifestyle.

Tap Water: A Modern Medical Crisis

Contaminated water supplies may have killed more people than any other single cause in history. When we hear about epidemics of cholera or typhoid fever in the world, contaminated water is to blame. Perhaps the greatest single public health achievement of history has been the creation of municipal water supplies that were sterilized with chlorine. This was pioneered in the early 1900's, enabling the rise of the modern American city. We are fortunate to have potable water coming from every tap. Sadly, just because you can drink American tap water without being acutely poisoned does not mean that American tap water is good for you. In fact, it is full of contaminants. One of the most dangerous ingredients in modern tap water is supposedly added for your benefit, and that is fluoride. Fluoride is yet another example of American industry hoodwinking foolish and arrogant medical professionals into accepting bad medicine on a massive scale.

163   Chester, J.G., Bremberg, M.G. and Reisacher, W.R., 2016, May. Patient preferences for route of allergy immunotherapy: a comparison of four delivery methods. In International Forum of Allergy & Rhinology (Vol. 6, No. 5, pp. 454-459).
164   Cox, L., 2015. Allergy immunotherapy in reducing healthcare cost. Current Opinion in Otolaryngology & Head and Neck Surgery, 23(3), pp.247-254.
165   Nurmagambetov, T., Kuwahara, R. and Garbe, P., 2018. The economic burden of asthma in the United States, 2008–2013. Annals of the American Thoracic Society, 15(3), pp.348-356.

In the 1950's, public health experts decided to put fluoride into the water. Fluoride was a hazardous by-product of aluminum production. Aluminum producers were anxious to dispose of it cheaply. What could be cheaper than selling it to the taxpayer? This was justified based on limited data supporting fluoride's role in preventing tooth decay. The level of evidence required before making this momentous decision on behalf of the public was, by modern standards, absurd. The entire country has been treated with fluoride for decades based on academic papers that would today have been hardly enough to justify mass-medication of the populace.

Fluoride is incorporated into your teeth and it is essential for their structure, but it is present in trace quantities. It is present in trace quantities in natural ground water. The form of fluoride in groundwater is also different to what is now added to municipal water. All of this calls into question the whole premise of water fluoridation as now practiced.

When fluoride was introduced to the water supply, we knew very little about its biological effects. Several decades later, studies have shown that fluoride lowers intelligence and causes anxiety. Rat studies repeatedly show this. Studies in children consistently show that the more fluoride children consume, the lower their intelligence.[166,167,168,169] Fluoride also inhibits the production of thyroid hormone.[170,171] Thyroid hormone is vital to life and longevity. Low levels of thyroid hormone used to be common, due to iodine deficiency. Iodine was then added to salt, and since then the incidence of severe iodine deficiency has dropped to virtually zero. Since the fluoridation of water began, low thyroid hormone levels have become a common medical problem, particularly among women. Patients routinely report that when they stop consuming fluoride, they need less thyroid hormone.

Fluoride has known toxic effects, even at the concentrations present in municipal water. Why are we still adding it to our water supply? Dentists are relentless in promoting fluoridation of public water systems, but even if

166   Till, C., et al. (2020). Fluoride exposure from infant formula and child IQ in a Canadian birth cohort. Environment international, 134, 105315.
167   Das, K., & Mondal, N. K. (2016). Dental fluorosis and urinary fluoride concentration as a reflection of fluoride exposure and its impact on IQ level and BMI of children of Laxmisagar, Simlapal Block of Bankura District, W.B., India. Environmental monitoring and assessment, 188(4), 218.
168   Green, R., et al. (2019). Association Between Maternal Fluoride Exposure During Pregnancy and IQ Scores in Offspring in Canada. JAMA pediatrics, 173(10), 940–948.
169   Razdan, P., et al. (2017). Effect of Fluoride Concentration in Drinking Water on Intelligence Quotient of 12-14-Year-Old Children in Mathura District: A Cross-Sectional Study. Journal of International Society of Preventive & Community Dentistry, 7(5), 252–258.
170   Kheradpisheh, Z., et al. (2018). Impact of Drinking Water Fluoride on Human Thyroid Hormones: A Case- Control Study. Scientific reports, 8(1), 2674.
171   Malin, A. J., Riddell, J., McCague, H., & Till, C. (2018). Fluoride exposure and thyroid function among adults living in Canada: Effect modification by iodine status. Environment international, 121(Pt 1), 667–674.

fluoride is effective for dental health, what effect is it having on our minds? Or the rest of our bodies?

When we consider all of the other elements we could add to our water, the standard for fluoridation becomes absurd. We know that higher levels of magnesium, calcium, and potassium protect us from many diseases, including heart disease, the number one killer in America today. We know that the higher the level of lithium in your drinking water, the lower your risk of death by suicide. All of these minerals are safe and have no side effects in trace quantities, yet we are not adding them to our water.

Public health experts refuse to accept that water fluoridation is a mistake. They refuse to reconsider the science, despite an abundance of evidence contrary to their dogma.

While public health experts staunchly defend fluoridation, they completely ignore dangerous contaminants that are not filtered out by their water treatment systems. American water supplies are contaminated with chlorine, fluoride, nitrates, lead, aluminum, bromate, cadmium, carbofuran, sulfonamide antibiotics, volatile organic chemicals, phthalates, pesticides, microcystin, giardiasis, dichlorofluoromethane and aminomethylphosphonic acid (AMPA) just to name a few.[172] All of this could be mitigated by more sophisticated filtration technology. The recent crisis of lead poisoning in Flint, Michigan is merely another chapter in the failure of America's public health experts to protect the public from water contaminants. Thousands of years after the ancient Romans were struggling with lead poisoning, American public health experts are still struggling with it. Do you really want to trust your water quality to these people? They can't even protect you from a problem we have known about for over two thousand years. I rarely quote or give credence to the New England Journal of Medicine anymore, but the title of one of their articles on the lead poisoning in Flint does the issue justice: "Lead contamination in Flint - an abject failure to protect public health."[173]

Lead is just the beginning. Fluoride is a much bigger story, and who knows how bad the rest of the common contaminants of American water supplies really are.

Eating Ourselves to Death: How Big Food Is Poisoning Americans

---

172   https://www.health.state.mn.us/communities/environment/water/contaminants/index.html
173   Bellinger, D.C., 2016. Lead contamination in Flint—an abject failure to protect public health. New England Journal of Medicine, 374(12), pp.1101-1103.

Americans have never had a worse diet than they have today. Public health officials will readily admit this, but what do they do about it? They blame patients and consumers. They come up with ridiculous ideas like taxing soda. Does it make sense to tax something that you are paying people to produce? Farmers are paid to produce corn. This drives the price down. The corn is then reduced into high fructose corn syrup, the main sweetener in corn syrup. This makes soda extremely affordable.

The high sugar content of the American diet is but one of the problems that the public health establishment chooses not to solve. Ironically, it is the most important public health issue they may be faced with. Before complex laboratory testing, physical examination by a physician, or expensive imaging, the single best indicator of your overall health may well be your weight and blood sugar levels.

What else in our food is poisoning us? The list is long, and some of it is being added for your supposed benefit. It includes, in order from farm to table, pesticides, herbicides, fungicides, food additives (including flavor enhancers, natural and artificial flavorings, colorings, and preservatives), and iron. Yes, you read that correctly – the nutrient, iron, is being added to our food and it is poisoning millions of Americans.[174]

Pesticides, herbicides, and fungicides (hereafter referred to as "pesticides") are used to prevent crop destruction by pests, weeds, and fungi. The number of pesticides rapidly expanded during the Green Revolution. The advent of genetically-modified organisms allowed Big Food to engineer crops that could withstand ever increasing quantities of pesticides. The result is that pesticide use in the United States has been rising over the past hundred years.

The earliest pesticides were based on lead and arsenic, developed in the late 1800's. These chemicals were in fact linked to the earliest epidemics of polio, leading many of us to question the viral origins of polio. The greatest use of DDT coincided with the worst polio epidemics the country experienced. This explains why so many breakthrough polio cases occurred in vaccinated populations, and why polio virus is found in people all over the world, but only causes crippling paralysis in populations exposed to toxic chemicals.

The increased crop yields afforded by pesticides enriched farmers and food manufacturers alike. No one wanted to blame them for epidemics of disease. It is much more convenient to blame an invisible enemy that you can only see with a scanning electron microscope, and that you can then engineer countless drugs to "treat." People who are spending all their money on these

174   Moon, Jym. Iron: the most toxic metal. George Ohsawa Macrobiotic, 2008.

prescription drugs often have no choice but to eat unhealthy food, because it is all they can afford. This is how Big Food and Big Pharma create problems for each other to solve.

Pesticides exert an insidious effect on our bodies. They accumulate slowly, without causing obvious disease, but they can still contribute to premature aging and disease. We may never know the true extent of damage caused by pesticides. What we can be sure of is that we are using more than we need to in modern farming methods. We do not need pesticides to feed the world. This is a falsehood peddled by Big Food. Pesticides have driven up food yields, driving down food prices, but only for foods that are unhealthy. If we feed the world with foods that are dependent upon pesticides, we will be unable to afford the healthcare costs that will result from such a diet. We do not need to eliminate pesticides, but the current increases in use are unsustainable. Pesticides are poisonous to humans as well as pests. They are suppressing the prices of foods that are then fueling our unsustainable healthcare costs. This is all due to the government subsidization of these crops. This is a problem that should be solved by freedom, rather than more laws, rules, and regulations. The public health establishment is busy shilling for the pharmaceutical industry, rather than addressing the root of the problem – the standard American diet.

Pesticides have destroyed the structure of the traditional American farm. Just a few generations ago, the average American farmer would have raised a variety of vegetables, fruits, grains, legumes, and nuts. He would have pastured goats, sheep, cattle, or chickens on his land. He would have hunted deer and boar. He would have fished ponds, lakes, and rivers for fish. Rotated crops through fields, to preserve soil fertility. Manure was the main fertilizer. This gave him and his family a diet with an abundance of micronutrients. He also had a variety of physical tasks to perform every day. He did not sit for hours atop a tractor or a combine.

Pesticides and artificial fertilizers seemingly obviated the need to rotate crops. With greater yields and government price fixing, farmers could make the most money by focusing on one crop. This has led to more and more problems over the years, because all that farmers have focused on is yield. Yield is considered in terms of weight or volume, not in terms of nutritional content. The food we eat (both animals and plants) has therefore been selectively bred for yield. We can easily see the difference in flavor. Compare an heirloom variety of any food to the cheapest version you can find at the grocery store. The color, consistency, taste, and even smell are different. Why is this? Taste comes from the complex arrangement of proteins, fats, carbohydrates, vitamins, and minerals that food contains. The higher the density of these nutrients, the stronger the flavor. Modern food has been bred to be bigger and bigger, but this means that you have to eat more and more of any given food to obtain the same content of micronutrients like minerals and vitamins. This is one reason why I see low levels of minerals and vitamins in so many of my patients. Repleting these nutrients with appropriate dietary changes and supplements can be life-changing.

Farms that raise a variety of foods naturally minimize pollution. Manure is valuable, because it is a ready source of nitrogen. There is a limited amount of waste, which is readily disposed of by sunlight, animals, insects, and microbes. Factory farms, by contrast, produce so much waste and pollution that it is overwhelming the environment. I am not referring to global warming, which at this point is obviously politics masquerading as science. To make matters worse, certain states have passed laws that favor certain types of farms. This results in extremely high concentrations of animals or cropland in certain states. For example, North Carolina raises approximately 12% of all of America's pork. Those pigs produce tons of sewage that does not require any kind of sewage treatment. It is left to rot in lagoons, spread on farmer's fields, or buried in the earth. There are communities all over America where the stench of rotting manure is present all day and all year. These communities should be expected to have higher rates of respiratory diseases, like asthma. There have been cases of well water contamination resulting in severe bacterial infections. Meanwhile, farmers in the Midwest are paying for fertilizer made from petrochemicals, instead of using manure like their grandfathers did. Large corn and soybean farms in the Midwest are producing so much water pollution that there is now a "dead zone" in the Gulf of Mexico, where fish now struggle to survive. This is an inefficient system. It is profitable only because the government is propping it up.

I find it ironic that the public health establishment is now focusing on climate change. If the public health establishment understood the first thing about environmental health, they would make the reformation of American agriculture their first priority. They are currently blaming cows for rising levels of methane in the environment. The cows are not the problem, the way their waste is disposed of is. If you spread manure over a large enough area, it breaks down rapidly and produces little if any pollution. The obvious solution to America's agricultural pollution is to stop subsidizing foods that are unhealthy, and return to a system where farmers can make a living growing a healthy variety of food. This will minimize pollution, while providing Americans with nutritious food at an affordable price.

After food has been harvested, it is processed. Food processing involves adding or removing things from foods. Sadly, we tend to remove what is most nutritious. White flour has had the brown "husk" of the seed (wheat, rice, etc.) removed. This husk contains B vitamins and minerals that are essential cofactors for the utilization of the carbohydrates found in the grain. This imbalance between micronutrients (vitamins and minerals) and macronutrients (carbohydrates, proteins, and fats) eventually causes diseases, most notably diabetes and obesity. Two thirds of Americans suffer from one or both of these illnesses. This disease starts with food processing.

What we add to our food is just as much a problem as what we remove. One of the first things I advise patients to remove from their diets is food additives. Food additives include natural and artificial flavorings, preservatives, and colorings. Food additives have a wide range of effects upon our bodies. These effects vary from person to person. For example, one person may develop a headache after eating or drinking certain foods. This may be related to an additive, such as sulfites or monosodium glutamate (MSG).[175] Yet not everyone develops a headache after eating these foods. Does this mean that these ingredients are safe?

I believe we should be free to consume what we want to consume, and to pay for the consequences. I also believe that if the government is going to mandate and control food labeling, then they should make it transparent. Food manufacturers can easily deceive the public with regard to what they put in their food. For example, many different ingredients can include MSG. You may purchase a food that does not list MSG as an ingredient, but that nonetheless contains it. They do this by hiding it under another ingredient, like natural or artificial flavorings. There are dozens of ingredients that can contain MSG.

Many diseases are the result of hidden reactions to ingredients in our food, which is why when many people eliminate certain foods or ingredients from their diet, they see major improvements in their health. Headaches, abdominal pain, anxiety, depression, joint pain, and more may all disappear when you eliminate the right food. The trouble is that there are so many additives that can be labeled as so many different things, that elimination diets are extremely difficult. The solution is to start with raw ingredients and cook at home.

Do we need food additives? Many of them are harmless. Who is to say which ones should be banned and which ones should be declared safe? The underlying problem is that the government is making the raw ingredients for

175   Niaz, K., Zaplatic, E., & Spoor, J. (2018). Extensive use of monosodium glutamate: A threat to public health?. EXCLI journal, 17, 273–278.

processed food incredibly cheap. If they stopped subsidizing commodity crops, the processed foods that contain the majority of food additives would become more expensive. American eating habits would shift to whole foods, rather than processed foods.

I believe that people should be free to eat whatever they want. The federal agencies that govern our food production – the FDA and USDA – have been completely compromised by their relationship to the industries that they regulate. Whatever regulation is necessary can be left to the states. Sadly, Big Food has plenty of political clout such that cheap, unhealthy food continues to be subsidized even as it kills millions of Americans each year prematurely.

One of the most toxic food additives in American food is also a nutrient – iron.[176] Most people are unaware of the fact that iron, while being an essential nutrient, is also highly toxic when present in excess. The question is then what constitutes an "excess." Iron is essential to many physiological processes, but is most well known as the critical component of hemoglobin. Iron deficiency anemia, or a lack of red blood cells, has historically been a major problem for humanity. This is due to the sheer variety of ways in which we lose blood, and the fact that blood loss is lethal. We lose blood to traumatic accidents, parasites like hookworm and malaria, and women lose it during menses and childbirth. We are so well adapted to surviving blood loss that we have no way to excrete iron. All iron that is absorbed by the body is retained by the body. This leads to the accumulation of iron within the body over time.

Iron deficiency anemia is one of the most misunderstood diseases in modern times. Most physicians think that iron deficiency is common, but few physicians realize that iron utilization and movement around the body is dependent upon vitamins A, B-6, B-12, folate, and trace elements like copper.[177,178,179,180] The diagnosis of iron deficiency only requires blood levels of iron that are low relative to the reference range. However, when blood levels of iron can be low, total body iron levels can be normal. Determining total body iron levels is possible, but it requires a liver biopsy. Magnetic resonance imaging (MRI) may one day prove useful to determine total body iron, but it has not been well studied for this.

176   Koppenol, W. H., & Hider, R. H. (2019). Iron and redox cycling. Do's and don'ts. Free radical biology & medicine, 133, 3–10.
177   Semba, R. D., & Bloem, M. W. (2002). The anemia of vitamin A deficiency: epidemiology and patho-genesis. European journal of clinical nutrition, 56(4), 271–281.
178   da Cunha, M., Campos Hankins, N. A., & Arruda, S. F. (2019). Effect of vitamin A supplementation on iron status in humans: A systematic review and meta-analysis. Critical reviews in food science and nutrition, 59(11), 1767–1781.
179   Mwanri, L., Worsley, A., Ryan, P., & Masika, J. (2000). Supplemental vitamin A improves anemia and growth in anemic school children in Tanzania. The Journal of nutrition, 130(11), 2691–2696.
180   Fishman, S. M., Christian, P., & West, K. P. (2000). The role of vitamins in the prevention and control of anaemia. Public health nutrition, 3(2), 125–150.

While many people may have low total body iron (we do not know exactly what proportion of those with "iron deficiency anemia" actually have low total body iron), many people develop iron overload over the course of their lives. The most extreme syndrome of iron overload is known as hereditary hemochromatosis, caused by a mutation in a gene that regulates iron absorption.[181] As iron accumulates, it begins to create oxidative stress. This contributes to premature aging and diseases like dementia,[182] obesity, diabetes, cardiovascular disease,[183] and cancer.[184] Patients with double mutations for hemochromatosis often die in middle age. The majority of people with a hemochromatosis mutation only have one mutation and often go undiagnosed. Those with single mutations will still accumulate iron faster than those without mutations. This puts these patients at increased risk of iron-overload associated diseases.

In the 1950's, public health experts advocated for adding iron to flour in order to treat low iron levels in the general public. This effectively poisons those who have single or double mutations for hemochromatosis. For the rest of the public, only a small proportion actually have low blood iron levels, and even fewer have lower total body iron. We do not know how much disease iron fortification of our food supply is causing, but there is every reason to believe based on the literature on iron overload and metabolism that it is substantial. There is no good reason to continue fortifying the nation's flour with iron. The public health establishment is slowly poisoning Americans with iron and, as with all their other failed interventions, they refuse to reconsider their advice on iron fortification of food. You may well be carrying a gene predisposing you to iron overload, in which case you are being poisoned by America's public health experts.

Energy and Public Health: The Failure of Gross Materialism and Mechanism

Since the dawn of medicine, doctors have argued about the role of energy in health and disease. Doctors and scientists on one side have minimized the role of energy in health and disease. They stick to biochemistry, looking at factors like toxins, infectious microbes or parasites, and nutritional deficiencies. They readily admit that energy, in some forms and quantities, affects life. No

---

181   Crownover, B. K., & Covey, C. J. (2013). Hereditary hemochromatosis. American family physician, 87(3), 183–190.
182   Ndayisaba, A., Kaindlstorfer, C., & Wenning, G. K. (2019). Iron in Neurodegeneration - Cause or Consequence?. Frontiers in neuroscience, 13, 180.
183   Kobayashi, M., Suhara, T., Baba, Y., Kawasaki, N. K., Higa, J. K., & Matsui, T. (2018). Pathological Roles of Iron in Cardiovascular Disease. Current drug targets, 19(9), 1068–1076.
184   Jung, M., Mertens, C., Tomat, E., & Brüne, B. (2019). Iron as a Central Player and Promising Target in Cancer Progression. International journal of molecular sciences, 20(2), 273.

one can argue that "energy" as something like sound or light cannot ruin your sleep. But this still leaves many questions unaddressed. What kind of emotional energy should a doctor bring to their encounter with a patient? Does cell phone or bluetooth radiation cause cancer? If so, then how much is necessary and how should it be regulated as a form of pollution? Does artificial light at night cause cancer? If so, what should we do about it? Should we ban the neon lights of the Las Vegas strip? Or force your cell phone to shut off at 9 o'clock at night? Clearly, different kinds of energy have a profound effect on public health. The question is what we should do about it. In general, doctors and scientists in American medicine, and American public health, look at disease as a malfunction of the biochemical and anatomical mechanisms of life. They do not emphasize the power of energy in the causation of disease or the maintenance of health. This school of thought is known as, "mechanism."

Mechanism has been at war with a competing doctrine, called, "Vitalism," for generations. If mechanists maintain that life is most of all about biochemistry and anatomy, then vitalists maintain that energy is integral to both and must be addressed as comprehensively and thoroughly as matter. Einstein's equation has two sides of equal weight, after all. Vitalists have been hamstrung by the fact that, until recently, our ability to measure many energies has been limited. Today, your cell phone can measure light and sound in your environment, and you can purchase simple meters that measure electrical, magnetic, and radio or microwave radiations in your environment for a few hundred dollars. The result is that we can now measure and correlate symptoms and signs of disease with energies in the environment in a way never before done in history.

This has become a cornerstone of my practice and has impressed upon me the vital nature of energy to health and disease. The vast majority of doctors and scientists today, and particularly those in the public health establishment, operate in ignorance of this new and emerging data. This is what gives doctors like me an edge over those who are limited in their knowledge to the effects of drugs and surgeries. This is why, as Americans have inundated their environments with new and artificial energies, their health has deteriorated, despite the fortunes they continue to spend on their health and medical care.

The failure to appreciate the power of energy is arguably the single greatest failure of American public health in history, though few have the perspective to understand why. Light, electromagnetic pollution, and sound are issues of vital importance to public health.

The Hazards of Artificial Light

In 2007, the World Health Organization recognized artificial light at night as a risk factor for cancer. This is one of the only public declarations from a public health institution to recognize and raise awareness about one of the greatest health hazards of modern times.

More and more people are coming to realize just how dangerous fake light is. This new awareness has emerged not thanks to the public health establishment, but independent experts and business owners. An industry has sprung up dedicated to helping people optimize their light environment. We have tirelessly explained to people how important fixing their light environment is and our message has spread far and wide via social media.

The public health community has also ignored the health benefits of light, particularly sunlight. We need light to be healthy, let alone happy. Many diseases increase in incidence and severity as we move further and further away from the equator.[185,186,187,188] These diseases are linked to a lack of light, particularly during the day, when we are supposed to be in bright light.

While excessive sun exposure leads to skin aging and skin cancer, it is vital to health. The Melanoma in Southern Sweden study demonstrated that the people who spend the least time outside have the same risk of death as those who spend the most time outside, but smoke. What we can infer from this is that, particularly in cold, dark latitudes, sun avoidance is a similar risk factor for death as smoking. Public health officials took decades to recognize the dangers of smoking. They are taking just as long to recognize the dangers of artificial light.

Meanwhile, dermatologists are busy warning everyone about the dangers of sun exposure. They do not even seem to bother reading their own literature. There are many caveats to the tired advice to, "wear sunscreen." Certain sunscreens contain chemicals that may well cause skin cancer themselves.[189] Strong light may make these chemicals even more toxic. This is

185   Mohr, S. B., Garland, C. F., Gorham, E. D., & Garland, F. C. (2008). The association between ultraviolet B irradiance, vitamin D status and incidence rates of type 1 diabetes in 51 regions worldwide. Diabetologia, 51(8), 1391–1398.
186   Hughes, A. M., et al. (2011). The role of latitude, ultraviolet radiation exposure and vitamin D in childhood asthma and hayfever: an Australian multicenter study. Pediatric allergy and immunology: official publication of the European Society of Pediatric Allergy and Immunology, 22(3), 327–333.
187   Grant W. B. (2010). An ecological study of cancer incidence and mortality rates in France with respect to latitude, an index for vitamin D production. Dermato-endocrinology, 2(2), 62–67
188   Simpson, S., Jr, Blizzard, L., Otahal, P., Van der Mei, I., & Taylor, B. (2011). Latitude is significantly associated with the prevalence of multiple sclerosis: a meta-analysis. Journal of neurology, neurosurgery, and psychiatry, 82(10), 1132–1141.
189   Matta, M. K., et al. (2019). Effect of Sunscreen Application Under Maximal Use Conditions on Plasma Concentration of Sunscreen Active Ingredients: A Randomized Clinical Trial. JAMA, 321(21), 2082–2091.

why the literature on sunscreen is mixed – some studies show a benefit, others do not. The idea that the sun causes skin cancer is overly simplistic. There are many other factors at work. If the sun causes skin cancer, then spoons make people fat.

Light is vital to good health. Public health experts have failed to recognize this, let alone raise awareness of it.

Electromagnetic Radiation

The health effects of electromagnetic radiation is one of the most fiercely debated topics in modern medicine. American public health guidelines were initially developed in the early Cold War. The standard was based on how much energy would heat living tissue, effectively "cooking" it. This is how much energy your microwave oven uses to heat up food. This is an enormous amount of energy. At the time, the only microwave and radiowave devices the average person had were a radio and a microwave oven. The amount of microwave and radiowave radiation coming out of your cell phone is many, many times what is emitted by your microwave oven or a two-way radio.

The health effects of electromagnetic fields are well-documented, even if they are not well-recognized by the public health establishment. Why, then, have public health experts failed to warn us about them? Scientists undertook the first major studies of the health effects of electromagnetic radiations in the years after World War II. During that time, the world's militaries were entering the Cold War. Telecommunications were vital to state security and to victory on the battlefield. The United States military could not afford to abandon wireless radiation as a means of communication on the battlefield.

Meanwhile, the telephone, radio, and television were revolutionizing American life. People love instant communication and entertainment. No one wanted to believe that there could be health hazards associated with watching too much television, operating a radio, or spending too much time on the phone. In the beginning, exposures were minor, simply because of the limitations of technology. Today, the exposures are massive and the health effects are becoming increasingly hard to ignore.

This has not stopped modern telecommunications companies from brainwashing Americans into thinking these energies are completely harmless. They have funded many studies to manufacture the illusion of safety. The negative health effects of wireless radiation, not to mention artificial light, are of great concern to Big Tech. Their profits depend upon proving that electromagnetic radiation is safe. Compare this to smoking. A generation ago, smoking was common because it was perceived as safe. Over the past several decades, this illusion of safety has evaporated. As it has, people have virtually stopped smoking. It is unlikely that Big Tech will see its revenues evaporate like Big Tobacco did, but it is possible that something like that will take place. Social codes, such as putting your phone on airplane mode when not actively using it, having timers to turn off wireless routers at night, or only having internet access via a hardline all reduce technology use and would be disastrous for the profits of Big Tech.

There is an abundance of literature on the negative health effects of electromagnetic radiations. The books, "Going Somewhere," by Andrew Marino, PhD, JD, "The Body Electric," by Robert O. Becker, and "The Invisible Rainbow," by Arthur Firstenburg, provide all the proof you could want. Sadly, America's public health experts have yet to read and act upon this information.

Sound

Sound pollution is perhaps the most under-appreciated threat to health, yet there is an abundance of literature demonstrating that excessive sound exposure is hazardous to health. We know that trains, planes, and automobiles create enough noise to impact the health of those living near train tracks, airports, or busy streets. There is controversy surrounding the safety of wind turbines, which create "infra-sound." As soon as wind turbines started to go up, people began to complain of new illnesses. Many of them noticed that these illnesses disappeared when they left the area of the wind turbines. Some experts dismiss these associations as an example of what is known as mass psychogenic illness (which we will address shortly). Others argue that these illnesses are real and that there need to be some safety standards around sound pollution. The public health community has done little, if anything, to raise awareness about sound as a hazard to human health. They do nothing to educate the public as to the fact that even mild sound pollution can significantly disrupt sleep. This job is left to clinicians like myself. I routinely identify noise disruption of sleep as a health issue, which means that it must be rampant among the general public. Yet public health officials do nothing to inform the public of this. They are busy promoting whatever makes money for hospitals and drug companies, rather than what truly prevents disease.

More Harm than Good

This is just a small sampling of the public health failures of the past several decades. There are many, many more, from Tony Fauci's handling of the HIV/AIDS epidemic to COVID-19. Stories of corruption and malfeasance have filled book after book, many of them referenced previously. Enough is enough. From our air quality to our food quality, America's public health experts have failed to protect public health. They are certainly not "following the science." They are, at best, dimly aware of the science, and then they choose only to give credence to the science that supports their failed policies. They are the acme of failure. It is time to abandon their advice and defund their ridiculous public health campaigns that do more harm than good.

9. Socialism Is Poison

Why Freedom Is the Antidote to America's Healthcare Crisis

"Today's scientists have substituted mathematics for experiments, and they wander off through equation after equation, and eventually build a structure which has no relation to reality."

- Nikola Tesla

Movement enthusiast Erwan LeCorre describes most modern people as, "zoo humans." When animals are caged in a zoo, they tend to develop strange and mysterious diseases. The best known example is probably "dorsal fin collapse," a phenomenon in which an orca whale's dorsal fin (the fin on the back or top of the orca) collapses. When you look at the average modern person, with stooped shoulders or swayback, we can easily see why they have become this way. Why do people settle for this state of health?

Why do we need to be free to be healthy? Imagine your natural state. You have next to nothing. You have simple tools and the use of your body. What can you do? You have to walk or run wherever you go. You have to hunt or forage your own food. You have to make all your own decisions. You have no one providing for you. You have no one to rely or depend upon but yourself.

What came of this state of nature? For most of our history, we have been petty, warring tribes who have barely survived the rigors of nature. Only in modernity have we removed ourselves from basic challenges of life like hunger, dehydration, or exposure to the elements. What happens when we remove ourselves from having to face these challenges? We get soft, weak, sick, and we die young. Facing the stresses of life is what makes us strong. When we remove stress from people's lives, we make them weak.

Not long ago, the average family grew, hunted, or foraged their own food, cut their own firewood for heat, repaired their own home, drew their own water from a well or nearby spring, and produced their own clothing. Few people were in a position to pay someone else to feed, clothe, house, or otherwise care for them. Only with technology has productivity increased so radically that suddenly the majority of people are engaged by a single job all day, everyday.

When you live close to nature, you are constantly exposed to new and dynamic problems. The weather is never the same from day to day, month to month, or year to year. One year you're figuring out how to deal with a drought, and the next you're worried about flooding. In the morning you might be hunting wild game, but you might be gardening in the afternoon. You naturally have a wide variety of tasks that demand a variety of different faculties. This creates a varied and diverse diet. The result is extremely resilient, physically fit people.

What happens when you do the same task over and over again? Consider the modern office worker. They sit at a desk, hour after hour, day after day, year after year. The caricature of the modern office worker is a sad, weak little drone who knows how to take orders. They have a limited ability to think for themselves, lead, or take risks. This kind of environment engenders obedience and conformity, not creativity, independence, or self-reliance.

The productivity of the industrial revolution gave rise to a new phenomenon in society - mass media. The first job of the media? To sell products that would support their production costs. There is a saying in marketing: "If you get something for free, you are the product." Have you ever seen a television commercial for growing your own food in your backyard? Catching your own fish? Hunting your own meat? Of course not. The closest thing you will see are advertisements for hunting, fishing, and gardening supplies or gear. These are hobbies that people engage in for fun - they do not need much advertising. There is much more money to be made selling people food, clothing, shelter, and other commodities than there is in selling them self-reliance and self-sufficiency.

How do you sell more products? You cut the costs of production and increase the amount of money you spend on advertising. How do you cut production costs? You compromise quality. This became rampant in the industrial revolution. People in modern democracies reacted to this by electing politicians who promised to protect their interests. They promised laws that would punish companies for deceiving and abusing the public. They also elected politicians who made public what might have otherwise been private. Sewer systems, roads, health insurance, the training of doctors and nurses, the approval and quality control of drugs and medical devices, and water treatment systems are all examples of public enterprises that are failing the public. Modern sewer systems in America are woefully inadequate. When it rains too much, they often dump raw sewage into waterways. Our road system is one of the best in the world, but it is also choking our inner cities with toxic air pollution. Medical devices and drugs are often approved only to be recalled later due to safety concerns. Moreover, many devices and drugs are proven, after approval, to be ineffective. Drug companies and medical device companies have no incentive to be honest when they control the regulatory agencies that approve their products. There are no consequences for the bureaucrats who hold power over these vital functions of society. Elected officials come and go, but the bureaucrats that run America's vital infrastructure and regulatory agencies remain the same. This is why America's infrastructure and health are crumbling at the same time. This is why American life expectancy is declining despite record spending on healthcare, let alone public health and medical research.

When you give the government control over any aspect of life, corporations immediately begin to capture regulatory agencies in order to take advantage of their powers. This is known as regulatory capture. Imagine if you are a major pharmaceutical company and suddenly the government creates a new office that regulates the approval of drugs. If you control that office, you can stop your competitors from competing with you. This is far easier than actually creating a superior product or doing a superior job of bringing it to market. This is why there are so many laws in our country. They are being passed by corporations to protect their interests, not yours.

Health Insurance Is a Scam

"The more corrupt the state, the more numerous the laws."

- Tacitus

Health insurance is perhaps the most egregious example of corporate capture of the state that there is. Consider the following questions with regard to health insurance, and I think you'll quickly realize just what a corrupt game it has become.

Why can't we buy and sell health insurance over state lines? We do it with car, home, life, flood, renter's, and more, and yet we cannot sell health insurance across state lines. If every other kind of insurance is sold across state lines, then wouldn't it make sense to sell this one across state lines too? Insurance companies could make more money, serve more customers, and have greater financial stability.

Why doesn't your health insurance company work to make you healthier? Did you ever stop to think that if you die, your health insurance doesn't lose a cent? Your life insurance company foots that bill.

What if your life and health insurance were the same thing? After all, you don't have two kinds of insurance for your car. Whether your car is totaled or just damaged, you have one insurance policy for it. What would happen if your health and life insurance policy were the same?

Why is your health insurance purchased through your work? Wouldn't it be nice if you could take it with you? Just like your home, car, boat, renter's, flood, or life insurance?

If health and life insurance were the same product, the company would have every incentive possible to ensure that you lived a long time and required as little medical care as possible.

If I could, I would start such a company. I would provide health and life insurance together, and I would incentivize you to participate in research that would serve you, by prolonging your life. I would give discounts to customers who would provide me with their data, such as is routinely being collected by consumers using fitness trackers. I would give discounts to customers who would provide me with their lab results. Then I would compare that data with the healthcare expenditures of my customers. We could thus determine how much any given dietary choice, exercise regimen, sleep routine, and so on, affected their health. We could see which zip codes were the healthiest, and which were not. We could see long-term public health threats before anyone else. I would also un-bundle health insurance. You don't want birth control? You don't have to pay for it, or anyone else's. You want us to cover acupuncture? You get to pay for it. Have you ever wondered how effective acupuncture is at prolonging life? How about yoga? Tai Chi? Fish oil supplements? Health insurance companies could study all of this to answer these questions, and they could get their subscribers to pay for it.

Imagine having a health insurance company that told you how to live your best life. Imagine someone informing you, based on real world statistics and outcomes, how expensive your health would be depending on your zip code, what time you get up in the morning, how late you stay up at night, how much exercise you get in a week, how many times you have sex in a month, how many times you eat fish each week, and much more. The sky is the limit for the kind of research the health insurance companies could do.

Instead, they abuse consumers to maximize profits. What most patients do not realize is that health insurance companies have little incentive to drive down their prices and provide better service. Why? They want to make sure that you are as sick as possible (without actually dying), because that maximizes the amount of money they can charge you for a policy. In a normal market, a competitor might come along and undercut their prices. Why doesn't this happen with healthcare? The answer is that the government stops entrepreneurs like me from doing this. They pass laws that protect the insurance companies from competition. I can buy car insurance from dozens of companies right now. I can barely find a single healthcare plan, even as a healthy, single young man who is employed. They charge me a fortune for providing me with next to nothing. Matters are worse for women, older individuals, and families.

Another reason that health insurance is so expensive is that you can walk away from your health insurance whenever you change your job. That means that any amount of time or money that your health insurance company might put into improving your health is value that you can take to another health insurance company. If they bother to do the kind of studies that I have mentioned above, their competition could simply copy their results, undercut their prices, and steal their customers. If you could invest in your health insurance policy the way you invest in a life insurance policy, you would not just walk away from it. This would incentivize them to invest in you.

Why don't health insurance companies provide incentives to be healthier? What if they gave you an incentive to lose weight? Quit smoking? Normalize certain lab values, like vitamin D or high-sensitivity C-reactive protein levels? They could do any of these things, but they choose not to. In some cases, the government will not let them. They say it is, "discrimination." This is nonsense. They are just encouraging people to continue living in mediocrity, rather than reach their full potential.

The other reason health insurance companies charge such high prices is that they are covering an enormous amount of medical care that people do not even want. For example, cancer doctors start treating cancer with "first-line" chemotherapy. This has the greatest likelihood of curing the person's cancer. The second-line is less likely to work, and so on and so forth. We have fourth and fifth line chemotherapy agents that are not curing anyone, yet health insurance companies are paying for them. Why? These agents tend to prolong life (we think) by a few weeks at best. Their side effects are horrific. I understand the desire to live a few more weeks, but on the other hand, many of us would never want to suffer through the side effects of chemotherapy. Why are we forced to pay for someone else's fifth line chemotherapy? Likewise, many consumers do not wish to be kept alive on life-support. Their medical bills may be hundreds of thousands or even millions of dollars less than those who do.

People who bring up issues like this are usually depicted as heartless misers who don't value human life. I am not herein voicing my opinion on how much care we should provide to cases that are incurable or hopeless, I am merely saying that no one should be forced to pay for another person's healthcare. Who decides what healthcare is necessary? How many lives would be saved if we spent all the money we currently spend on chemotherapy on advertising campaigns for fruits and vegetables? Or if we just bought nutritious food and shipped it to starving children all over the world? Authoritarian thinking in healthcare (forcing people to pay for the care of others) opens the door to corruption, agency capture, and the poison of socialism. Those who paint people like me as heartless misers merely want to avoid uncomfortable conversations about the realities of human nature. They want to force us to submit to their authority and rule, often by manipulating us with guilt, shame, and fear.

Health insurance is a scam. Medicare and Medicaid are no better. Medicare and Medicaid do nothing to improve the health of those who use them, they simply encourage those people to be completely dependent upon them to pay their medical bills. Ironically, Medicare and Medicaid reimbursement are so poor that most doctors struggle to make a living accepting them. They have to see more patients to make up the difference, which leads to more prescriptions, which leads to more profits for the pharmaceutical industry.

Socialized Medicine Is an Even More Evil Scam than Health Insurance

Socializing medicine further will not fix this problem. Why? Socialism does not work. History has demonstrated this conclusively. The temptation for many is to throw money at this problem and to make laws prohibiting people from being unhealthy, but this has been an obvious failure. The reason is that as soon as money is made available by the government for the purposes of promoting health and fighting disease, corporations start to repurpose that money to their own profits, rather than the service of public health. Cancer screening is an excellent example. We know that eating a healthy diet, and specifically limiting processed foods, is vital to preventing cancer. All of the money for cancer screening is funneled into vaccines, mammograms, colonoscopies, colposcopies, and serological testing for cancer antigens. It even gets put toward advertising for these procedures. Many of these interventions are of dubious value.[190] Little, if any, attention is paid to the importance of diet, lifestyle, and environment in the prevention of cancer, yet we know that diet, environment, and lifestyle all play a critical role in cancer prevention.[191]

We already know that socialized medicine does not lead to better health, because the people in America who already have it are some of the least healthy members of our society. There are five groups in America who qualify for government healthcare. They are veterans (via the Veterans Administration), government workers (specifically active duty military), the elderly (Medicare), the impoverished (Medicaid), and Native Americans (The Bureau of Indian Affairs). None of these populations is what we would call "healthy." Why? They are being set up to fail by the same people who claim to want to take care of them. It is much more important to pay attention to what politicians do than what they say, and in this case, what they are doing is damning evidence that they are (for the most part) morons and sociopaths.

What has convinced me of this? Look no further than American agricultural policy. Starting in the 1950's the Green Revolution made food so abundant that people started to become obese in large numbers. Decades later and we have epidemics of obesity and diabetes. At the same time, the value of the dollar has fallen, wages have not risen to make up the difference, and the average American is struggling to afford healthy, nutritious food. Just a few generations ago, the average American ate a local, seasonal diet of incredible quality. Today, Americans are so broke that a large proportion of them are on food stamps. Those who are on food stamps are, as a rule, overweight or diabetic.

"Give them bread and circuses, and they will never rebel."

- Juvenal

What are the number one and two purchases with food stamps? Junk food and soda top the list. There is no debate among serious physicians, scientists, or public health experts that junk food and soda are unhealthy. This

---

190   Myers ER, Moorman P, Sanders GD. (2016). Breast Cancer Screening: Benefit or Harm?—Reply. JAMA. 315(13):1402–1403.
191   Irigaray, P., J. A. Newby, R. Clapp, Lennart Hardell, V. Howard, L. Montagnier, S. Epstein, and D. Belpomme. "Lifestyle-related factors and environmental agents causing cancer: an overview." Biomedicine & Pharmacotherapy 61, no. 10 (2007): 640-658.

is not a partisan issue, yet it is one that goes completely unaddressed every single election cycle by the mainstream media. Where do you think that food stamp money goes? It goes into the pockets of food manufacturers, who pay large agricultural corporations and conglomerates for the raw materials they need to turn raw food into processed food. Some of the money makes it to farmers, but they are not the ones profiting from this arrangement. In fact, farmer suicide rates and bankruptcies have reached record highs in recent years. Much of the money finds its way into the hands of large agricultural corporations. These corporations are a monopoly; they engineer the seeds, pesticides and the fertilizers that farmers have come to depend upon.

What do the large corporations that control the American food supply do with all this money? They fund political campaigns so that they can control politicians, and then use that power to improve their profit margins.

There are three ways to destroy your competitors politically. The first is to enact taxes or fees on their businesses. The second is to take money from the tax-payers so that you can undercut their prices. The third is to pass laws that will force your competitors to spend money complying with. Modern corporations are rampantly destroying our freedoms and enriching themselves using all three of these strategies. Food stamps again provide the perfect example. Big Food bribes politicians to tax consumers into poverty, which leaves them looking for the cheapest food available. They then pass bills subsidizing the production of junk food with the tax dollars. Then they make it impossible for small producers to compete by passing laws that require them to spend money to comply with regulations. The most frequent excuse is, "food safety standards." This is how the American government and American corporations are turning the United States into a failed socialist state. This is not a free market - it has aptly been named crony capitalism.

The laws of basic economics dictate that as there are more and more customers with more and more resources to purchase a given good or service, there will be more and more businesses offering those goods and services. That is why a hundred years ago there were numerous small farms across America. Today, there are few small farms left. They have been replaced by large farms that are all beholden to major corporations. The family businesses that existed alongside these small farms have been wiped out. They have been replaced by giant corporations. Competing with these corporations is virtually impossible - they have written the laws in their favor. There is nothing fair about this - it is the worst kind of corruption imaginable. The deck is stacked against the average American in every way possible, and it is only getting worse.

The Government Is the Problem

"We have the best government that money can buy."

- Mark Twain

The government could easily enact policies that provide small farmers with an adequate living, instead of living on the verge of bankruptcy. They could stop providing subsidies for crops that are literally poisoning the American people, like corn. They could start providing subsidies for fresh fruits and vegetables. They could stop letting people buy junk food and soda with food stamps. They could only allow them to buy fresh produce, meat, or seafood instead. They could transform the American diet and the health of this nation overnight.

They could do all of this with the stroke of a pen, and yet they do not. And we are expected to believe that these people care about feeding the poor? This is absurd. They care about selling the poor food that is unfit to eat. They care about keeping them indoctrinated via social media, so they will not question who to vote for. They care about keeping the poor in such a state of ill health that they are all on prescription medications. Big Food is being paid to poison America and the Big Pharma industry is being paid to suppress the symptoms of this crime, while Big Tech runs cover for both.

I came to these conclusions after years of working as a traveling doctor. I worked in hospitals from Florida to Maine to Minnesota. I worked primarily in places that no one wanted to live full-time, which is why they needed a traveling doctor. This meant that I worked predominantly with the impoverished. For two years, I worked on the borders of three Native American reservations in Northern Minnesota. I was struck by the fact that my tax dollars paid for their healthcare, much of their food, and that casinos paid for much of their expenses otherwise. Despite this, many Native Americans live in abject poverty. They do not become educated and go on to enjoy prosperous careers. They struggle with epidemics of drug abuse, alcoholism, and sex-trafficking. This is despite the vast sums of money that flow into them every single year in the form of food, medicine, and pure cash. The idea that more laws and more money will fix these problems is one of the most pernicious lies in history.

How were the Native Americans reduced to this state of existence? First, they were deprived of their natural sources of fresh, local food. Then, they were fed preserved foods given to them by US government officials. They were forced onto reservations, where their natural way of life was impossible. They were sold alcohol, processed food, and all the comforts of modern life. A few hundred years later, and the reservations are some of the most bleak, unhealthy places in the United States. This is despite the fact that much of their food and medical care are provided for them by the United States government, or by tribal revenues from casinos. Native Americans have immense wealth as a result of their casinos, but they have been unable to buy back the good health that their ancestors enjoyed when they had not even the means to mint coinage, let alone print paper money.

What could be more tragic than being so wealthy that you cannot buy back the good health you had when you were poor?

We are told that the "health disparities" within our society are due to discrimination by certain ethnic groups against other ethnic groups. This avoids the uncomfortable fact that the government has fueled these disparities, and continues to do so. The ethnic groups in America who "enjoy" the least government benefits also enjoy the best health statistics.

What is more dangerous to life? The freedom to fail and starve in the wild, or the freedom to cash checks written by the government for toxic food, mediocre medical care, and addictive tech devices? I would personally and professionally suggest the latter.

Many people have been tempted to pass laws that force people to be healthy. Cities like New York have taxed sugary beverages. Consider, for a moment, the absurdity of this. New Yorkers are paying taxes to the Federal government that are then sent to farmers to produce corn, which is then used to make beverages that New Yorkers then pay taxes on.

Why not just stop the subsidies and let the price of sugary beverages rise as a result? Many intellectuals are proposing increasingly farcical laws that will "force" people to be healthy. These morons do not seem to understand that the real problem lies not in having enough laws, but in having too many of the wrong sort of laws already. All laws passed for the benefit of human health are ultimately twisted to its destruction.

The truth is that people want to be healthy. They do not need subsidies, hand-outs, or incentives. They do not need to be coerced. They just need to be free to make their own choices, and they will sort out how to make it happen. They also need to be forced to accept the consequences of their own actions. They need to be prepared to pay for what they want. I have seen patient after patient who ate garbage every day for their entire lives and then expected the tax-payer to foot their medical bills. How is this just?

Americans must reckon with the simple fact that as they have accepted more and more free food and free medical care, they have steadily become sicker and sicker. This is not a secret - it is an inarguable fact. Doctors, scientists, and government officials are viciously defending this status quo in an effort to save face. They look like a collection of imbeciles and sociopaths for having let things get as bad as they are, and they are desperate to remain in their positions of power in society. They realize that their incomes are entirely dependent upon the illusion that spending money on things like food and healthcare will improve the state of the average American. That illusion is wearing thin. Few people capable of independent thought are still falling for it.

Freedom is the answer to our modern healthcare crisis, not more laws, subsidies, or mandates.

10. Liberty or Death

How to Reclaim Our Rights from Totalitarian Technocrats

"There is no justification for taking away individuals' freedom in the guise of public safety."

Thomas Jefferson

In October of 2020, Twitter censored Doctor Scott Atlas, a physician with impeccable credentials and academic achievements. Martin Kulldorff, a professor at Harvard, remarked, "After 300 years, the Age of Enlightenment has ended."[192] Twitter has since censored countless medical doctors, scientists, and citizens, all in the name of public health. The scientific progress of the West, including its immense infrastructure and exceptional quality of life, has depended upon the free exchange of ideas, no matter how heretical or seemingly erroneous. We are now at risk of falling into a new dark age. Our Constitutional Republic is at risk of being transformed into a totalitarian technocracy - a state in which experts act as dictators to the public at large. This is what the Great Reset is all about. The Great Reset, an initiative of the World Economic Forum, is an agenda to remake our society according to the will of the same totalitarian technocrats who brought us the ugly medical authoritarianism of mask and vaccine mandates. We all know how poorly mask and vaccine mandates have worked out - who in their right mind would trust these same people to remake the global economy?

What is happening today in science in the West happened in Soviet Russia. In the early years of the Soviet regime a Soviet geneticist named Lysenko became a close ally of Stalin. He used his power to denounce scientists whose theories contradicted his. Time has proven these scientists correct, but this did not help them at the time. Lysenko held show-trials and had many of these geneticists put to death. It would take generations for Soviet genetic research to catch up to their Western counterparts. In 1962, the Nobel Prize

---

192   https://twitter.com/martinkulldorff/status/1317768803862839301?lang=en

in Medicine and Physiology was awarded to James Watson, Francis Crick and Maurice Wilkins for the discovery of the genetic material – DNA. On April 14th, 2003, the Human Genome Project was completed. In the span of a single human lifetime, we discovered the genetic material, learned to manipulate it, and sequenced the entire human genome. During the same time period, virtually no significant genetic research emerged from Russia. Russia controls one sixth of the world's land mass. The population of Russia in 1945 was approximately 170 million and is now approximately 144 million. It is home to many distinguished scientific institutions, and the Russian people have made many great contributions to the world of science. The evil actions of one scientist almost a century ago crippled Russian progress in one of the most important fields of science for generations. [193]

This should never happen again, but many of us fear that it may.

In the West, by contrast, scientific freedom has been the rule of law for centuries. People have been free to believe what they want to believe, and they have never faced political persecution or reprisals for it. This has changed radically, particularly since the emergence of COVID-19. American scientists are not being lined up before firing squads – yet – but the rhetoric being leveled at scientists and physicians is increasingly hostile. Where does this end? The reality is that there is no evidence that lockdowns, masks, and vaccines provided any benefit. There is substantial evidence of harm. How can anyone in good conscience shame those of us who believe that freedom is more essential to public health than anything else? We have ample evidence to support our beliefs.

The Modern Day Scientific Censors

"Whoever would overthrow the liberty of a nation must begin by subduing the freeness of speech."

- Benjamin Franklin

Peter Hotez, MD, PhD, has recently called for the silencing of what he calls, "far-right wing" politicians. These "far-right wing" politicians are publicly elected officials, empowered by citizens to represent their interests and fight for their rights. If politicians are no longer allowed to criticize scientists

---

193   Lerner, K. Lee. "Lysenkoism: A Deadly Mix of Pseudoscience and Political Ideology." Academia, https:// www. academia. edu/39758097/Lysenkoism_A_Deadly_Mix_of_Pseudoscience_and_Polit ical_Ideology (2001).

and physicians, who will be allowed to criticize them? Drs. Anthony Fauci and Francis Collins of the National Institutes of Health have echoed his sentiments. Evidence has emerged that they even took action to attack those who disagreed with them.[194] State medical boards and specialty boards have made similar statements. What they are proposing is the end of freedom of speech and freedom of religion. The only acceptable speech would be speech that is acceptable to people like Hotez. Once men like Hotez have control of what people can and cannot say, science will cease to progress in vital areas, and may even regress. Private corporations will continue to take control of the organs of government that are empowered to police our speech, and gradually eradicate all dissent. This must not be allowed to happen.

I would describe Hotez as a totalitarian technocrat. These people have extensive technical expertise, but they are repeatedly wrong in their predictions of what will happen. Despite being wildly wrong over and over again, they insist that they should have unprecedented control over society and individuals.[195] They believe their opinions are more important than the social contract - the United States Constitution and the Bill of Rights.

What crime does Hotez accuse men like Rand Paul and myself of? Only that we do not subscribe to his scientific paradigm. We do not accept as true things that he considers to be true. We are distrustful of data that he chooses to trust. His recommendation to silence us stands in stark contrast to the rule of law in the West for generations. In modern times, silencing someone effectively means deplatforming them, or depriving them of unrestricted access to the internet. If tomorrow, Google, Facebook (and its subsidiary, Instagram), TikTok, and LinkedIn decide that someone is a threat to society, and deprive them of the use of their platforms, that individual will effectively lose all one online revenue. Rand Paul and I are guilty of what George Orwell called, "thoughtcrime." He wishes to destroy his political and ideological opposition, in direct violation of the laws of this country.

Today, the American government is paying American pharmaceutical companies billions of dollars to secure contracts to vaccines that do not even work. In fact, these vaccines are, according to many experts in the field, extremely dangerous. This is why over 16,000 doctors and scientists have signed a declaration opposing the continued use of these vaccines, and the mandates that are driving people to undergo vaccination.[196] The government is neglecting basic fundamentals of drug safety research. They are shielding the companies

194   https://www.aier.org/article/fauci-emails-and-some-alleged-science/
195   Taleb, Nassim Nicholas. The black swan: The impact of the highly improbable. Vol. 2. Random house, 2007.
196   https://globalcovidsummit.org/news/watch-talks-from-leading-physicians-at-the-florida-covid-summit

from litigation. Government scientists are in bed with these corporations, and now many of those scientists are trying to silence their opposition, both politically and scientifically. Government officials, scientists, doctors, and the pharmaceutical industry are ignoring deaths and injuries that are obviously the result of these vaccines. Whistleblower after whistleblower has come forward attempting to expose the deception of the pharmaceutical industry and the corruption of our government. Our government has become subservient to private corporations, using its agency and power to protect those corporations from embarrassment and liability. The corporations then fund the campaigns of the dominant political party, ensuring their continued hegemony. This is a recipe for a one-party dictatorship.

Americans see this and cannot help but be distrustful of it. The undercurrent of vaccine hesitancy is growing from a trickle to a torrent, but the full depth of this movement is not visible within the medical community, because men like Hotez are so viciously intolerant of those who disagree with them on this topic. I know only a handful of physicians who are publicly opposed to vaccination, let alone forced vaccination. I know far more physicians who have chosen not to stand up and oppose this agenda, for fear of losing their livelihoods.

The Key to Scientific Progress Is Freedom

"So much of left-wing thought is a kind of playing with fire by people who don't even know that fire is hot."

- George Orwell

The key to scientific progress in the West has been freedom. Historical precedent clearly shows us that when we stifle scientific research between consenting adults, false scientific paradigms can come to dominate society. The temptation to pick and choose who to suppress and who to elevate is attractive only to sociopaths, narcissists, and useful idiots. Eventually, industry will always corrupt those with such absolute power over human thought. This must not be allowed. To suppress the speech of others over a difference in opinions of science is a clear violation of the First Amendment. It will lead to exactly the social problems that plagued the Soviet Union under Stalin, Germany under Hitler, and that still plague China and North Korea to this day.

Americans must wake up to the reality that they are being exploited and rapidly enslaved by their government and their most profitable industries – Big Food, Big Tech, and Big Pharma. They must reclaim their ancestral rights and restore law and order within the nation's borders. They must stop the corporate welfare that is killing them, the war on small businesses that is impoverishing them, the war on independent doctors that is depriving them of good medical care, and the politicization of science that is making it virtually impossible to know where politics end and scientific research begins. The alternative is to devolve into a third-world country, where only the ultra-rich can afford decent food, healthcare, and recreation.

More and more Americans are waking up to this reality. They realize that life, liberty, and the pursuit of happiness are synonymous with freedom. We cannot be healthy, wealthy, and happy, without being free. People like Peter Hotez want to sell you unsound and unsafe solutions to problems that are the inevitable result of authoritarian policies. We must reclaim our republic and our liberties from the grasp of petty tyrants like him.

Andrew Breitbart said, "If you can't sell freedom, you suck." Americans have never been more passionate about being free. They have never been more animated and excited to return to the principles upon which the country was founded. The chickens of authoritarian policies are coming home to roost, and millions of Americans are realizing that freedom is the only solution. The challenge before us is to extricate ourselves from a system that is trying to enslave us.

This is a blueprint to achieving freedom from that system.

Stop Consuming Big Food's Unhealthy Products

We have become dependent upon other people, often in other countries, for our food. This is insane. Packaged, processed food is driving epidemics of modern disease. When you start buying local food and preparing it yourself, you will see your health change. As more and more Americans do this, we will see our communities change. Family farms and farming in general used to be a unifying force in America. As farms have turned into giant factories, we have seen life in rural America stagnate and decline. Americans must become self-sufficient again, and they must begin eating local food and preparing it themselves for this to happen.

Deplatform Big Tech

Big Tech is deplatforming exceptional Americans like Laura Loomer,[197] Alex Berenson,[198] Steve Kirsch,[199] and many more, whose only crime is to tell it as they see it. This censorship is wrong. We must deplatform Big Tech. They have done enough damage as it is. Not only are they corrupting the public discourse and opinion, they are rotting people's minds with their highly addictive and dangerous algorithms that distract them from the real substance of life.

Fortunately, platforms that support free speech are gaining traction. The ones that I am using are Telegram (t.me/stillmanmd, Substack (stillmanmd.substack.com), and Rumble (https://rumble.com/stillmanmd). I am also registered for Gettr, Parler, and Gab, all with the username StillmanMD.

Opt-Out of the Corrupt Health Insurance Scam

Health insurance is a scam. Giving those people your money is bargaining with the devil. The time has come to opt out of these plans in every way possible. Health sharing ministries are a great option that everyone should explore. High-deductible plans are the best option for most healthy, young people - use the money you save to invest in your health.

I have re-invented my practice over the course of 2022 to meet the needs of all Americans. My goal is to empower and educate you to need as little medical care as possible. This is a tough business model for a doctor, but it is honest work.. To become a patient at my practice, fill out the brief application on my website, StillmanMD.com. To stay up to date with what I and other doctors are doing, I encourage you to subscribe to my Substack and Telegram channels.

Get Started with Dr. Stillman

The greatest threat to your health and wealth right now is misinformation mistaken for marketing. Health "education" you receive for free is almost invariably misinformation mistaken for marketing. Someone is paying for the videos, photos, and clever slogans that eventually convince you to buy gadgets, gizmos, pills, potions, or powders to protect yourself from disease. Health

---

197   https://lauraloomerforcongress.com/
198   alexberenson.substack.com
199   https://stevekirsch.substack.com/

insurance, as we have discussed, is not insuring your health at all. If you are investing more money into your car or home each year, without understanding and optimizing your health, you are making a long-term financial mistake. The number one cause of bankruptcy in this country is medical bills. If you want to avoid medical bankruptcy, you need to work with a doctor who understands how to prevent disease. A doctor who can teach you how to be and remain healthy, no matter how corporations or the government try to poison you next. You deserve great medical care, and that is what I offer my patients at my practice. I am currently licensed in Florida, Virginia, and New York, and am seeing patients in-person in Florida. I offer virtual services to patients who see me at least once yearly outside of these states, and if you don't want to travel to see me, you can work with myself or a health coach on my team to improve your health virtually. If you do not invest your time and money into your health education, you will wind up in a statistic used to sell life insurance policies.

Apply to become a patient at my website, StillmanMD.com.

Defend Your Freedoms

Freedom is not free, and now more than ever, it requires you to show up and fight for it. You must vote for candidates who will fight for your freedom, and against candidates who support the expansion of the government and the restriction of your liberties. You must be prepared to fight in new and unconventional ways if you are going to win this fight. The ballot box is not sacred. Campaign promises are not contractual obligations – they are empty promises until they are fulfilled. You must hold politicians accountable and destroy them when they betray you. There can be no room in a functional republic for politicians who sell out their constituents. What they are truly selling is your health and your wealth. You must not let that kind of betrayal go unpunished.

Sign up with your local health-freedom activist groups, specifically Health Freedom for Humanity and Freedom Keepers, to find out who to support to maintain our liberties.

Do Not Comply

Boycotting those who lack the courage to defend freedom is essential to preserving freedom. There are so many businesses and individuals who value freedom in this country that there is no reason to patronize those who refuse to defend freedom. If you live in a place where people do not value freedom, and find yourself having to patronize businesses that do not respect your rights, then it is time to move. Wherever you move, be prepared to fight for your rights, because just as they have disappeared in so many places, they can disappear where we still enjoy them. That must not happen.

Freedom Keepers is a national organization that is devoted to maintaining medical freedom and bodily autonomy. They are now maintaining a list of businesses that support health freedom, and who pledge never to discriminate against their patrons or employees on the basis of medical status or religious beliefs. Keep as much of your business as possible with pro-freedom businesses.

Blow the Whistle

I have spoken out time and again on social media, despite criticism and threat of censure by my colleagues. I spent two months undercover with Project Veritas in part to prove a point - you have no excuse for tolerating malfeasance and corruption. You must blow the whistle on corruption. You must be willing to risk everything. I have risked everything and I expect nothing less from you or anyone else. For every whistleblower who actually does something, there are thousands of people who are toiling away within the system who know they should do something, but choose not to. If everyone chooses to be a coward, then everyone will wind up as a slave. To blow the whistle, you need to become independent from the system, so that you can still make a living and have a life. This is why blowing the whistle comes last in this list. You need to be independent from the system to have the freedom to speak. That is the number one way they are controlling people, particularly healthcare workers.

Your Choices Determine Your Reality

The future of freedom rests in your hands. I hope you have enjoyed this book and that it has given you insight into why our world is so sick, and what you can do to set things right. You must now act. The future of the world if we all sit back and enjoy the last of our freedoms, rather than fighting to restore the Constitution, is bleak. I have taken every risk possible in the pursuit of liberty. I urge you to do the same. The risks I take, I take because I refuse to settle for slavery 2.0. I don't want anyone to live the miserable life that is the doom of those who buy into fake food, fake medicine, and fake news. Now is not the time (nor has it ever been) to take our freedom for granted. Now, and always, is the time to fight for it. In the words of James O'Keefe, "be brave – do something."

Beyond the fight at the ballot box for our freedom, there has never been a more important time to invest in your health. One of the greatest mistakes I see freedom-loving Americans making is neglecting their health. People need to realize that when you are unhealthy, you are not in command of your full mental faculties. You are susceptible to propaganda and coercion. This is why states that have the most authoritarian public health measures have the worst health overall. You need to learn how to breathe, drink, eat, move - how to live - a healthy life. It is not as simple as "diet and lifestyle." What exactly does that mean? As you can see from this book, I work with my patients to optimize every aspect of their diet, lifestyle, environment, and mindset. That is why I have come to expect exceptional results for my patients. What could be more valuable than good health? Everything else in your life can be abandoned, divorced, or sold. Your health is your only permanent possession, and your most important. The time to invest in your health is now. Become a patient at my practice today and start your journey to achieving the good health you desire.

Until then, be well.

Leland Stillman, MD

9 798986 009100